Gumboot Girls

Gumboot Girls

Adventure, Love & Survival on British Columbia's North Coast

*a collection of memoirs
compiled by Jane Wilde
& edited by Lou Allison*

CAITLIN PRESS ✳ HALFMOON BAY
2014

Caitlin Press
8100 Alderwood Road
Halfmoon Bay, BC V0N 1Y1
www.caitlin-press.com

Design by Chris Armstrong.
All images contributed by the writers.

Maps by Craig Outhet of Strait Geomatics.

Reproductions of cover images courtesy of Jean Eiers-Page at the Prince Rupert City & Regional Archives.

Photograph on front cover courtesy of Richard Fish. Pictured are (left to right): Shelley Lobel, Dolly Harasym, Nancy Fischer, Tosh, and Chloe Beam. A sketch of that photograph, drawn by Chloe Edbrooke, appears on page 1.

Image on back cover, entitled "December 21st, 4 p.m. 2006," is a batik by Betsy Cardell.

When the Night Was Young
by Robbie Robertson
© 2011 WB Music Corp. (ASCAP) and Point Conception Music (ASCAP)
All rights administered by WB Music Corp. All rights reserved.

My Back Pages
by Bob Dylan
© Special Rider Music. All rights reserved.

Printed & bound in Canada.

ISBN 978-1-927575-47-5

CATALOGUING DATA AVAILABLE FROM LIBRARY & ARCHIVES CANADA.

Table of Contents

the
N orth
C oast
of
British
Columbia

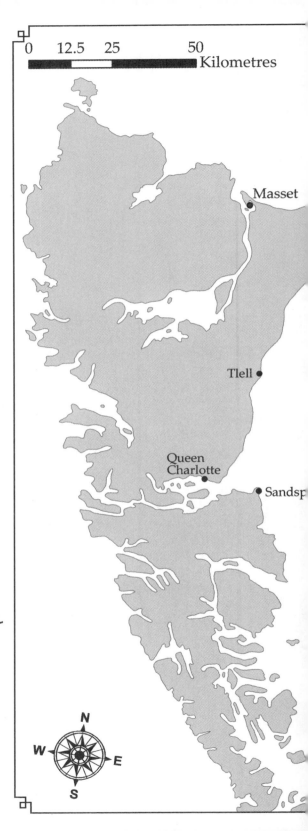

0 12.5 25 50
Kilometres

Masset

Tlell

Queen
Charlotte

Sandsp

N
W E
S

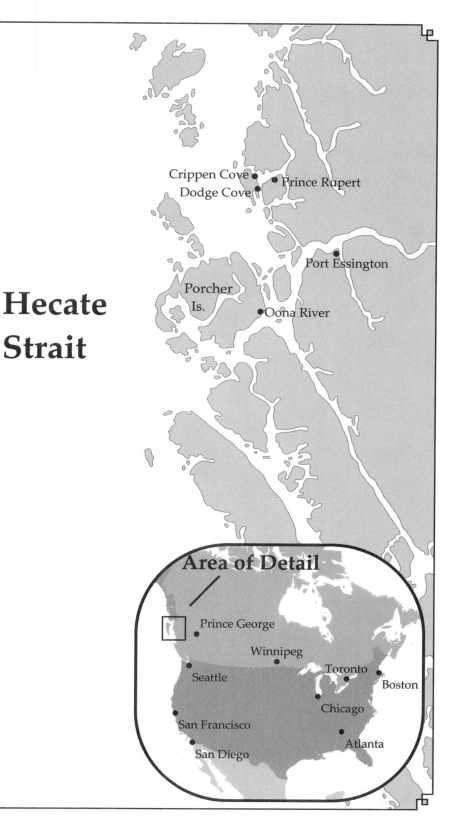

Hecate
Strait

Crippen Cove
Dodge Cove
Prince Rupert

Port Essington

Porcher
Is.
Oona River

Area of Detail

Prince George

Winnipeg

Seattle

Toronto

Boston

Chicago

San Francisco

San Diego

Atlanta

Introduction

Reading the book *Girls Like Us* by Sheila Weller, about Carole King, Joni Mitchell and Carly Simon and the influence they had on women all over the world through their music and lives, triggered a cascade of memories. I realized that my friends and I had also been part of the same shift in the roles and expectations of women that she described. I was intensely moved by Sheila's observations and her research of women's experiences in the 1960s and 1970s.

Until reading Sheila's book, I hadn't connected that as I was going from a teen to adult during the seventies, migrating from urban southern Ontario to the remote B.C. north coast, I was also taking part in a much bigger demographic shift. Many of us were living the shift and just didn't notice. We had opportunities that were new to young women, opportunities that our mothers, and even women reaching adulthood a decade earlier, had never experienced.

Unknowingly at the time, many of us were part of a women's movement that was offering women more life options, a sexual revolution that was freeing us to explore relationships in a new and less restrictive way, and, for some, a back-to-the-land migration that was also influencing our choice of destination and lifestyle. Communities of like-minded migrants were forming in rural pockets all over North America.

I thought about my own experience and that of the friends who came into my life at that time; I also thought of women I have met or heard of since. I wondered about the stories of other women like me, or, put another way, "girls like us." I felt that we shared a unique history that needed to be told, appreciated and saved. The idea of gathering those stories into a book took root.

I invited 11 women that I knew had also lived on the north coast in the seventies to write their story of those years. I also asked them to invite others of their friends to join us. Thirty-four writers eventually joined the group and this book project was launched.

Our writers are originally from all over North America, almost half from the U.S., and one from France. We were all young women who arrived on B.C.'s north coast in the seventies looking for adventure and love; along the way, we learned how to survive in the harsh northern environment. We settled around the shores of Hecate Strait, on Haida Gwaii (formerly called the Queen Charlotte Islands) on the western side, and on Prince Rupert and the surrounding islands on the eastern side. Many have lived in more than one community and on more than one remote island in this area.

The motivation for arriving in these places at this time varied but there were similarities. Seeking adventure and change drew many. There are a number who came because they had work as teachers. Jobs in the commercial fishing industry drew others to both the fish processing plants and the fish boats and, for a few, fishing became their career. For young women in the U.S., social and political upheaval and opposition to the Vietnam War motivated them to move to Canada, many with partners or relatives avoiding the unrest and the draft board. Some writers read in the 1969 supplement to the Whole Earth Catalogue that farming and self-sufficient living were possible on the Charlottes. House or boat building, and food self-sufficiency through fishing and gardening, became focuses for many. And, of course, romance: traveling north with men who were or who became partners, moving north to escape former partners, meeting men who became partners, relationships forming, breaking, reforming, lasting: all common themes.

Our informally chosen group of 34 writers represents a small sampling from the hundreds of young women who came to this area in the seventies, some to stay and build a life here, some to stay for a while and move on. Enduring friendships and connections were formed; families were started that are the bedrock of present lives. We have our own, unique, north coast version of a time that Sheila Weller called "magical and transformative."

~Jane Wilde
Prince Rupert, November 2012

Editor's Note

This project is Jane's brainchild. When she read *Girls Like Us: Carole King, Joni Mitchell, Carly Simon and the Journey of a Generation* by Sheila Weller, she caught fire. She managed to inspire us with her idea of writing *our* story, after we got over our initial reaction of "You think we should do *what?*" Not only is she an original and inspiring leader, she is a formidable organizer and, equally important, a lot of fun. Thank you so much Jane for your energy and vision.

It has been a privilege to edit these stories. As each crossed my desk, I read with a mounting excitement: every personality was so bright and vivid and every voice so individual. Though the approaches were different, many themes emerged, crossed and connected, expressing our shared experience: placing group food orders, gardening in the coastal climate, quilting together, changing or committing to partners, having children, running boats of all sizes, working hard at subsistence living, earning a livelihood, celebrating with feasts, potlucks, wild parties (and poetry), staying or leaving, and, most viscerally, connecting with the geography of this magical, mystical place.

I was pleased to note, as well, the cross-seeding of names scattered throughout. In less than 3,000 words, no one could name all her influences, friends or lovers, past or present, but names popped up here and there, underlining connectedness.

Also, another thread, a dark one, slowly emerged: the deaths of friends, lovers, acquaintances, and children. Some of the stories mention these deaths, some do not, but we all lost someone. Often that event precipitated a major change in our life. I hadn't realized that commonality before – which I hope this book honours – and I wonder how many other patterns will emerge as we read and share our story.

I feel honoured and privileged to be part of this project.

~*Lou Allison*

NOTE ON PLACE NAMES

The terms Haida Gwaii, the Queen Charlotte Islands, the Charlottes, and the Islands are used interchangeably by the writers. They all reference the same place. The blade-shaped archipelago off the north coast of B.C. was given its English name in 1787 by George Dixon, who surveyed the area for Britain and named it after one of his ships, the *Queen Charlotte*. On June 3, 2010, it became officially known as Haida Gwaii, meaning "place of the people" in the Haida language. Most of the action of the stories in this book take place pre-2010, so the writers call the place by its old name. In most cases, when talking about the past, the writers call it the Queen Charlotte Islands, and when talking in the present, they call it Haida Gwaii.

The terms Salt Lake and Salt Lakes are also used interchangeably by the writers. The official name is Salt Lake.

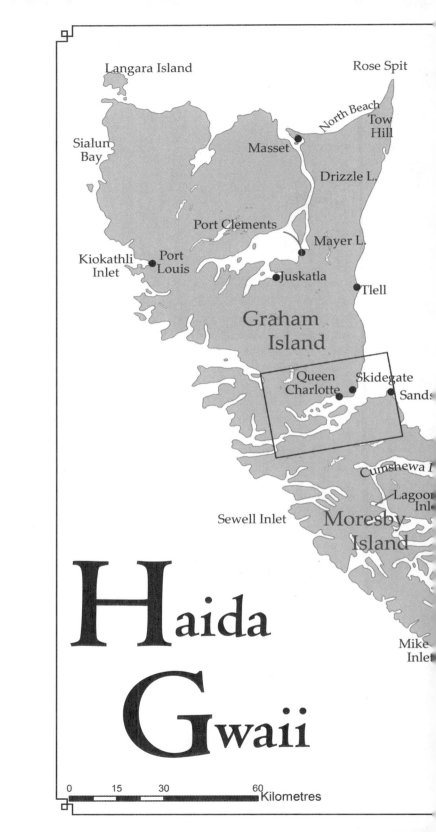

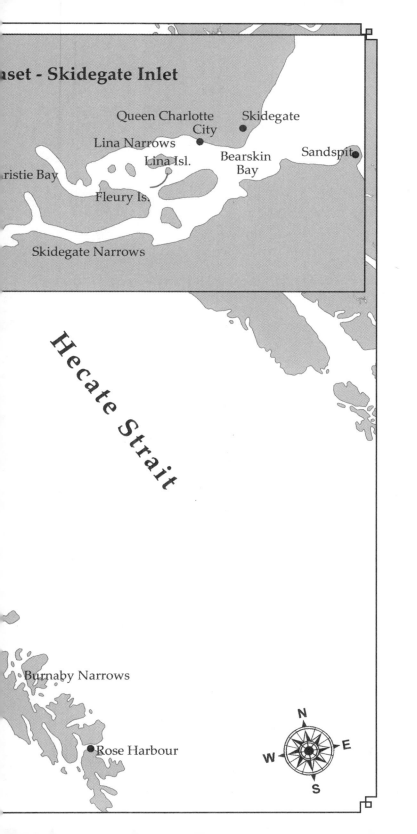

aset - Skidegate Inlet

Queen Charlotte City

Skidegate

Sandspit

Lina Narrows

Lina Isl.

Bearskin Bay

ristie Bay

Fleury Is.

Skidegate Narrows

Hecate Strait

Burnaby Narrows

Rose Harbour

N
W E
S

A Few Left Turns

by Carol Kulesha

I AM A NEW YORK CITY GIRL, born and bred for Bloomingdale's and sub-ways. Somehow I took a few left turns and, some 40 years later, live on a remote island off the northwest coast of British Columbia, in a town of 1,000 people.

The first left was not marrying a medical intern and instead taking my nursing degree to Ethiopia for a couple of years. Then I delayed my master's degree at U.C.L.A. and, instead, travelled the road to Kathmandu. I never did earn that degree, but I did meet Karl, my future husband, in Afghanistan. We landed back in the U.S. three years later. We tried a stint in Haight-Ashbury and farmed a few acres in Oregon for a summer, but we did not fit anymore.

So in 1970, with our vast experience farming, we decided to go back to the land. Consulting the *Whole Earth Catalog*, the bible of the day, we read an article about the Queen Charlotte Islands and the Haida people. The author said he was writing from jail but had hid out here with the "natives" and suggested bringing beads to trade. We didn't find much more information at our local library. Some friends had immigrated and were buying land in Sechelt but we wanted to see these mythical islands first. So, Karl cut his hair and we packed up our Volkswagen Bug with all our worldly possessions, including our two German Shorthair dogs and the chainsaw. Armed with a letter of promised employment from the Q.C. Islands General Hospital, we drove to the Washington border. It seemed we needed an appointment, so we went for lunch and came back to line up with the other Salvation Army suits and white-necked potential immigrants. After medicals and paperwork, we took our freshly minted documentation and camped our way across B.C. until we hit Prince Rupert. We shipped out on one of the Northland Navigation freighters to the Islands, sharing a cabin with some new friends while our car and dogs rode on the deck.

An acquaintance recommended finding Tlell. We saw the sign on the side of the road and a few miles later another sign exiting Tlell. After two more tries we understood that this was it. We were in Tlell! We set up our tent in the campground and began our island life. I still remember that first dinner: as much crab as I could eat, bread dipped in melted butter, and a bottle of wine. It's still one of my favourite meals to this day.

In truth we never expected to stay. People came here to work and retired "down south." My family was pressuring us to "find ourselves" and return. They offered to buy a trailer park in Florida and have us run it. That conversation took place in a phone kiosk and Karl picked me up from the floor after I collapsed laughing.

For a while we did house-sitting. When that grew old, we built a pole and shake cabin in Lawn Hill. Much to our surprise, someone owned the land and he called the police to remove us when we asked for permission to farm a piece. The provincial government was equally unimpressed. We applied for a chunk of the forest for agriculture and, fortunately,

Carol & Karl on their way to the Charlottes, 1970.

they never granted it. I was nursing part-time, which meant "whenever they needed me." As it turned out, they needed me a lot. It was interesting nursing. A single shift could range from dead boring to juggling multiple deliveries, emergency room casualties, and pediatrics. The bonus was that the hospital had a bathtub downstairs with all the hot water I could use.

It was obvious that Karl's university days were over so he needed to choose: forestry or fishing. It made sense that as we lived on an island we should have a boat, so we borrowed money and purchased our first fish boat, a 34-foot double ender, the *Alp*. Karl had been out sport fishing in San Francisco Bay so he was experienced. As for me, well, I inherited my father's stomach and threw up for the next seven years.

According to the laws of the day, we could not become citizens for five years. Though we could own a boat and work a boat, we could not captain a boat. Fortunately, a lovely young French girl came to work with us that first summer. Each night at Seven Mile we would tie up to the wharf and begin to replace the gear that we lost that day while helpful men crowded on deck to share their fish stories and help our captain. One day, it finally all came together. We had the hooks on the lures the right way, nothing was breaking, we were not entangled in kelp and, lo and behold, we caught fish. We were hooked.

Those first years we narrowly escaped death a number of times; the boat leaked but the planks did not give way; the engine coughed but did not fail; the pea soup fog lifted at 5 p.m. and we found our way out of the double circle set of crab traps; the weather fortuitously came down and we made safe anchorage; we found the harbour through the rocks. Slowly, through it all, we learned how to catch fish. By our second boat, the *Jay Mar*, we were making a living and by the third one, the *Fancy Free*, we were successful freezer-trollers. I gave up nursing in the winters so we could return to travelling. We explored South and Central America, India, and Southeast Asia. We always came back because Queen Charlotte had become our home.

I now have a house overlooking the bay and I watch the boats heading towards the Narrows and the west coast. We retired from fishing after 25 years. Commercial fishing is not what it once was, but I still like to talk the talk and hear the fish stories. When I entered the industry, the men did not know what to make of me. They wondered who the boy was throwing fish in at the back of the boat. Tying up boat-to-boat on a harbour day, they did not know if they should invite me on board like the captain or leave me with the crew. The government was similarly parochial. I was not allowed to collect unemployment insurance, as I was "working on my husband's boat" and the money we earned together to buy the boat was considered his. I had to open a separate savings account for my nursing income to prove I earned a salary and establish a line of credit. I was furious at the injustice and ever grateful to the farmers' wives who gained our equality. Selling fish was another battle. There was not much choice until we had a freezer. With 13 other vessels, we established a co-operative called Pacific Wild which marketed our fish as far as Japan and Europe. I was the treasurer, Karl the president. When we retired, the co-op had grown to 94 vessels and changed how troll fish were bought and marketed.

Then I took another left. A friend invited me to the Queen Charlotte/Skidegate Landing Advisory Planning Committee meeting. I didn't know what the committee was or did, but by the end of the meeting I found myself an elected member and stayed on when my friend quit a few months later. I was now in local politics. Karl the anarchist was appalled and he remained aghast for the next 14 years as I was elected to different levels of local government: from the Management Committee to the Regional District and eventually becoming the first mayor of the newly incorporated Village of Queen Charlotte in 2005. I am still living in Queen Charlotte, now serving my third term as mayor. I've learned the joys of a small town, the caring, gossip and interactions between all ages. I have met young women just arriving here, discovering Haida Gwaii, and I am impressed by their utter comfort in their equality, their total non-understanding of their inferior role! What a pleasure. I also work and play with some of the women I met in those early years, some whose sto-

ries are also in this book. Their long-time friendships are central pillars in my life.

I would say now that the rest of my life's path is set out before me, but who knows, there may yet be another left turn out there.

Carol & Karl fix the Alp.

Going North Again

by Jane Kinegal

I'M ABOARD A DASH 8 at the Vancouver airport, preparing to take off to Haida Gwaii. I've been making this trip up and down the coast for more than 40 years, and would venture to guess that I've done the journey more often than I've had birthdays: a mighty number from where the sun now stands.

The reasons I go back and forth, north and south, have not changed, but the circumstances have altered over time. My family — my daughter Quincey, her partner Cees, and her children, Nate and Clara Jane — pick to live in the south, in Vancouver, where I also enjoy my life. But when people say "welcome home" to me when I get to Haida Gwaii, my heart sings.

From my earliest days as a little kid, the Charlottes figured heavily in the fishermen's stories I heard in Sunbury, at the mouth of the Fraser River. Us girls and women and the younger men stayed home in the summer to work in the cannery, but the fishermen and a few lucky wives got to go up north to Rivers Inlet, Alert Bay, Prince Rupert, Masset: places that all sounded so wonderful. Before I got old enough to work in the cannery, I sometimes got as far as Mitchell Bay, on Malcolm Island, where my dad would drop me off with family friends on his way north to attend to fleet business in Rivers Inlet.

In the early sixties at U.B.C., I met two lovely men from Massett who were downtown recruiting teachers. I was a student in education, ready to go, and their quiet sales pitch started me dreaming of going north to see those far-off places I had only heard about. But someone tall, dark and handsome had a different proposal, so I stayed south and took a teaching job in Richmond.

In the late sixties, on the run from a very conservative situation, I answered an August ad for a job teaching art in a high school in Prince George. I crammed what I needed into my little M.G.A. and set off north, though way inland from what I was used to. After I got settled in Prince George, I still had three weeks till school started, so I followed my natural instinct to head for the coast. I took the train to Prince Rupert, explored the fish cannery, then boarded the *Northland Prince* to the Charlottes. We arrived in Masset at about 2 a.m., and I spent my first night on Haida land at the Singin' Surf.

I never did see the gentle recruiters, but maybe I wouldn't have recognized them without their suits. What I did see, that first morning when I took an early walk around the town, was a young guy, maybe 13 or 14, roughly half my age, who greeted me warmly — as if I belonged there. I have never forgotten that. In my experience, many young teens don't even see people outside their own demographic, much less flash them a gentle hello from their heart. I think that was the morning I also discovered the incredible banana cream pie at Don's Drive-In. I know for a fact that was the morning I met Bruno, a man I came to hugely admire, and watched with him as the Masset cannery burned down. Bruno was very upset, and I zipped off to find some brandy, which seemed required.

I had met a "mountain man" on the Northland boat who was heading out to the west coast of Graham Island to visit his friends Donna and Ken, who had recently moved from Prince George to settle in Sialun Bay. I was delighted to be invited on this visit, but maybe wasn't paying as much attention to the details as I should have been when the journey was described. I almost balked at the idea of flying in a tincan plane out of Masset to Langara Island, which turned out to be the first and by far the easiest part of the journey. The rest of the trip involved hitching a ride on a boat with some fish buyers near Langara, then walking, climbing, scrabbling up and down some very steep and high hills, lurching around on slippery black beach rocks, and generally getting much closer to Ma Nature than I ever expected to be in the three days it took to reach these pioneers.

I was some pleased at last to see an A-frame with a chimney smoking away, even if the roof was just made of heavy construction plastic. What I really wanted in the worst way was a cup of tea, which came right after huge and joyful bear hugs and warm warm greetings. I drank many cups of what turned out to be Labrador Tea, making my introduction to the back-to-the-land movement a very mellow affair indeed.

We visited for a few days in that edgy paradise, and when it was time to go, K.P. decided to walk back out with us. I made the return journey with a small kitten, who had surprised everyone by being born out there to the family cat, riding in a sling around my neck. Even though that slowed our travels, we made the 17 mile on-foot part of the journey in one day that time.

By the time I returned to Prince George, I had cooled somewhat in my enthusiasm to teach school. Though I had enjoyed my year in Prince George, it seemed natural and right to relocate to the Charlottes. On that first visit, a friend had driven me down from Masset to Queen Charlotte City, and I was smitten. I can still see the sign, "Queen Charlotte City – Unincorporated," that I saw on the way into town. After a splendid lunch at Margaret's, with an amazing crowd of locals, it became increasingly clear to me that I wanted to be one of these offshore islanders too.

The principal of the school in Prince George was a bit surprised when, in the first week of the school year, I told him I was resigning as of June 30. That was the year that paying into the Unemployment Insurance (U.I.) program became mandatory for teachers. When the U.I. representative insisted that I could not be exempt, I said it seemed like buying life insurance after the funeral. He was unmoved. When he told me I would never be able to claim U.I., I vowed to him and all the amused teachers at the meeting that I would indeed collect. So later, when I lived in Port Clements, near Juskatla, for a few months, I realized my promise. Now, really – who would hire a girl like me to be a chokerman? Living outside the monetary system, but with an infusion of U.I. funds, proved to be quite a treat. I think it was due to U.I. that I was able to buy the last lot on Hippie Hill from John, the legendary landowner, after our house burned down at Gold Creek – but that's another story.

The settler life at Sialun Bay ended abruptly and quite famously while I spent the winter teaching in Prince George. The details of the end of that venture are recorded in Kathleen Dalzell's book, *Of Places and Names*. At the Easter holiday, the mountain man and I, and K.P., and Paul, hired a small plane to drop us off in Port Louis on the west coast, to scout around for a new place to call home. We found Kiokathli Inlet (where Yahgulanaas' *Red* unfolds), which has to be one of the best places on Earth. We were stuck there for a few days longer than we expected, waiting for decent weather for the plane to come back for us. During those days, any doubts I had about living on the edge of the edge were completely erased. I grew to love the wild changes in the weather: rain, then snow, some hail, then gusty wind, then bright sunshine poking through the pearly clouds, then something else. Then something else again. I felt right at home in that raw and incredibly beautiful place.

When we started to build our lives in Kiokathli Inlet, it was a truly fine time and place to be alive. Our experience was sometimes coloured by what I thought were probably the usual tensions that arise when new lifeways are being created, but I would not have missed those times for anything. At its peak, the population of our little community reached 10 humans. I also made friends with a lovely little seal, who came daily to the rocks where I sat every morning at grey light, who would splash around and seem to scold if my attention wandered off. Kenny, Donna, Paul and Anita have passed on now, and I don't know what has become of the mountain man, but they all remain alive in my memories of that bright time, and many other times that unfolded after we all moved back to town.

We grappled with life lessons of the most fundamental kind out there together:

How do you bake bread? And how would you do that in an airtight? *I will always be grateful to Donna and Anita for the answers to the first question, and to the Kens for figuring out the five-gallon can and bricks inside the airtight heater trick.* How do you put out a cat that is on fire? *The cat figured that one out.*

Can a woman who has never been pregnant learn how to deliver a breech baby by reading a Guatemalan midwifery manual if the plane doesn't arrive in time? *The weather cleared up and the plane came.*

Do we really need tools? *Yes!*

Can territorial issues between men be resolved with humour and grace? *Sometimes.*

Is it easier for women to collaborate, and is smugness and pride appropriate if sophisticated relations amongst women are more readily achieved? *Yes. And no.*

Is home schooling possible with a 7-year-old boy who is living in the forest and possibly experiencing culture shock?
I wish I had tried much harder to discover how to do this.

Does town living prepare us for respectful bush living, and, if not, how can we figure out how to look after the land in all this freedom?
We were not always good at this and I am sorry.

Jenny sent a beautifully illustrated poem she made for Kenny and his family that was nailed to a pole rafter in their home. It said:

> Wind's blowing more
> Thinking about you vastness seekers
> Fierce old ocean mother
> Look after you.

We were very well looked after. We routinely ate like wealthy bankers, and everything we needed to make our haywired homes was there. When K.P. cussed and even shot a few bullets at the ocean the day the highest tide of the year flooded his home, I wasn't so sure we were all appreciating that abundance as graciously as we might, at least on that wet, rowdy and hilarious occasion.

In the fullness of time we left that privileged place and moved on to the rest of our lives. The seventies offered a seemingly limitless range of life choices and many of us permitted ourselves to explore that range with joy, and courage, and, likely, a sense of invincibility too. That sense, illusory or not, served us well at the time, and once formed, has probably continued to power subsequent adventures. O the seventies!

People often have asked me, "what did you actually do up there?" I used to answer that I made friends, visited, and drank a lot of tea. That was true, and it was a fine way to live, but when I look back over those years, I see that answer is incomplete. I was busy. Though the general stance was pretty relaxed, I had the opportunity to get involved in some very interesting and lively action. I learned to cook from scratch and to sew or knit or otherwise make anything we needed. Donnette taught me to crochet, which led to hats for many of my loved ones, and blankets too. I went dancing every chance I got: rocking to the tunes of incredible musicians on the Islands, and even Sufi dancing led by Stas. I also learned first-hand where shelter comes from by building a small but quite sturdy house. It had not been at all clear to me what was involved in making buildings, but I figured if I could sew, I could build with other materials too.

Because of my background in teaching, the superintendent asked me to set up a continuing education program in 1973, which involved meeting some wonderful people who had courses to offer, and I got to teach ceramics to adults in Port Clements and Queen Charlotte as well. I worked at the hospital as a lay counsellor, and helped organize and run our Charlottes Alcohol and Drug Society Support Centre in Tlell. The N.D.P. association was growing at that time in the north, and I had a great time organizing and campaigning for our national treasure, Jim Fulton, M.P. and Graham Lea, M.L.A. I became their constituency secretary when Jim was first elected in 1979.

Over time, I worked in a very satisfying variety of other jobs as well: at Margaret's, at the bar, cooking at the daycare, cleaning at the Hecate Inn, writing for the *Observer*, substituting and regular teaching at the school, flogging items at Art Dirk's second-hand store, and as deckhand/cook/wife on our troller/gillnetter. Sam Simpson invited me to work with him to edit a book called *Growing Food on the Charlottes*, and I did that in spite of the fact that I have never grown a vegetable. (I am pretty good at flowers.)

I missed studying and learning with others, so I got involved with the United Church, even attending Bible study classes led by Reverend Bob, who made our minds soar with his theological concepts. I took courses too: anthropology from Pinkerton, political science by correspondence from U.B.C., and drafting from the Ministry of Education – I had not been allowed to take drafting when I was in high school because I was a girl. The biggest and most important learning for me ever was becoming a mom. I had been invited to help at the births of several babies, an offer I had gratefully refused before Quincey was born, but which I embraced with joy after my own experience giving birth. I also loved being a member of the community of parents, which had been like a foreign country to me before Quincey came along.

Besides, or maybe integrated with all the social freedom, I personally revelled in the chance to live in different types of dwellings. I have always been very interested in social settings, and I mentioned earlier that I went north because I was on the run from a pretty straight setting: what I considered to be an unecologically small population of two people in a huge house in Kerrisdale. I loved living in our plastic and pole shack in Kiokathli Inlet. And it was great to live communally with a cabin full of fine friends and musicians in our fixed up and very picturesque trapper's cabin at Gold Creek. I lived for a while in a dome when that Gold Creek home burned, and then was offered the chance to live in a beautiful pleasure boat at the Queen Charlotte docks. I lived for a short time in a fishermen's cabin in Tlell, and in the architectural and historical gem owned by a Richardson in Port Clements, which eventually got moved to Tlell and became Donna's home. I spent three seasons on Hippie Hill in a homemade camper that was crouching on my lot, before I decided to build my own updraft double shed house there. It turned out to be 150 square feet, plus a loft, built with wood rescued from a demolished chicken house in Tlell, some shakes I got to split from bolts offered to me at North Beach, and several recycled true divided light windows given

Jane's updraft house, 1976.

to me by a generous soul. I lived on the *Child of the Moon* for five fishing seasons and shared that 150 square-foot home on the Hill with a 250-pounder, my husband Ken, in the off-season.

When my daughter was on the way, I regained my urge to live in a (relatively straight) home more suitable for raising a child. Bob, a local cabinet maker, built a little house according to my sketchy plans that served our family very well in various ways until we sold it in 1995. (I immediately started looking for another place in Queen Charlotte, and we bought a trailer with a view of Bearskin Bay a few years ago, perched up behind the former United Church building and the Thrift Shop.)

The process of designing and helping to build our home on the Hill had an ironic twist. I realized that the design/build process was the second most creative act I had ever been involved in; motherhood was the first. So I made the decision to go south to study and practise architecture. That is why we left our little home on the Islands, all those years ago.

Now, in the second decade of the new millennium, I look back with gratitude that I had the wit to join in on the wonderful plots that unfolded on the Islands in that free and generally magical time, with characters that were living so joyfully and so well. I left at the beginning of the eighties to go back to school and have subsequently envisioned and realized some goals that took years to incubate. But now, a new period of freedom is coming into focus. Quincey is grown and a dear friend; I have been squirrelling away all those Airmiles for more trips up and down the coast. I really should retire before I get too creaky. So what is next?

I boarded that Dash 8 in Vancouver to look at a jewel of a house that is for sale. It is not the Charlottes anymore, it is Haida Gwaii. And two women said "welcome back to Haida Gwaii" to me when I arrived, not "welcome home." Maybe I have been away too long. And I am no longer a young woman exploring the exciting and seemingly unlimited possibilities of the seventies on the north coast. I am almost old, enjoying the challenge of making an important decision about where and how I am probably going to spend at least a good chunk of the rest of my life. Some of my dearest friends have lived on the Islands for the past 40 years and I would love to finish growing old with them. The community has continued to evolve and to grow in ways that I respect and want to be part of. I am trying to make a decision based on a thoughtful accounting and the beating of my heart — godwilling that it continues to beat, of course.

If it does turn out that I do relocate to Haida Gwaii on at least a part-time basis, I am understanding that I would not be going back, but going forward, with old and maybe some new friends, to navigate the beautiful, sometimes choppy, ever-changing northern waters and paths. And I feel, now, just as fortunate as I felt over 40 years ago, to have the chance to make this place my home.

When the Wind Blows

by Joline Martin

THE EARLY SEVENTIES WERE a turbulent time in the United States. The Vietnam War, Kent State massacre, and the advent of free love had a huge impact on people coming of age. My peers and I, while enrolled in university, were also trying to figure out our place in the world. I decided my place was out of the United States of America, most probably Europe. I didn't want to support a government that had a propensity for blowing up little brown people. I just could not face being a part of such a country; I longed to be a part of a positive community where I could grow and change and make a significant social contribution.

While I was at university, my brother moved to the Queen Charlotte Islands. I missed him terribly and wondered why he moved to such a faraway place. Through our correspondence I learned more about the "Misty Islands," and I became fascinated with finding out what they were really like. So, on my summer break, I made a trip to the Queen Charlottes to see for myself.

British Columbia is a long way away from Illinois; even longer if you have limited funds. In June 1971, a friend was moving back to his home in Everett, Washington, so I was able to share expenses with him on the long drive until he was safely ensconced in his parents' home. From there I took a bus to Vancouver, where I slept in the airport until the flight left for Sandspit. I was the only female on the plane. The flight was uneventful, except for two loggers squabbling over beer. Landing was exciting, as the approach was over the water and the plane touched down close to the end of the spit. Transportation to Graham Island was provided by an old school bus which was parked outside the airport. It made its way down the road to the shore, where we boarded a barge and crossed the inlet. At the end of my five days of travel, my brother met me and took me to his log cabin.

Except for a few camping trips, I had never stayed anywhere without running water, electricity or indoor plumbing. Heat came from an air-tight stove stuffed with alder. We carried our water and lived a simple life, eating sardine sandwiches and cheddar cheese from Chapman's Store in Port Clements. And we had fun.

It was during this trip that I met Karl and Carol Kulesha, two people with whom I have a lasting and deep friendship. Carl and Julie were also soon to become good friends, and there were many others. That summer I learned how to skin and butcher deer, clean and fillet fish, chop wood, and kill a chicken. While none of these had been on my list of skills to learn in life, I found them immensely satisfying. I felt in charge of my destiny and I wanted more.

Returning to finish university that fall was difficult, but necessary. After graduating in the fall of 1972, I returned to the Charlottes for what I thought would be a year. The first few months I stayed with Carl and Julie, a kindness I will never forget. I was soon able to find work, a place to live and become a member of the community, with a little help from

Joline in her cabin on Haida Gwaii, 1976.

my friends. Life filled with social and community events as well as the chores associated with living in a small, rural town. I learned to make do with less or different things, shop for the week and get around without public transport. But these are not the important things I learned during those early years: they are just the practical ones.

Most of Illinois has been disturbed from its natural state, so I knew little of nature. I fell in love with the natural world. Gale-force winds made the biggest impression on me. I came to love the energy they brought to water and land. Moss beds so deep you could sleep on them fascinated me. Eagles' mating rituals in the spring captured me; I soon came to anticipate the return of their air show each spring.

While Mother Earth surrounded me, I dug deeper into her realm in my daily living. There is a saying on the coast: "When the tide is out the table is set." I am not sure of the saying's origin, but I do understand the meaning. I quickly learned to dig clams of all sorts, net for crabs and pick mussels from rocks. The sea also provided fish, a source of protein I had not eaten before due to its poor quality and availability. Mushrooms, berries and seaweed also became part of my diet. I grew closer to the natural world and loved every minute of it.

For a time I did some teaching at the local school, mostly substituting. It was there that I met Betsy Cardell. We shared a lot of interests and quickly became friends. At the time, I was living at Karl and Carol Kulesha's, house-sitting while they were out on their boat fishing or travelling in exotic places. Betsy was renting a house a few doors away that belonged to the school board. Later that year, Jane Wilde, a young woman in long whirling skirts, began teaching home economics at the school: she was blonde, buxom and a great cook. Our little circle of friends included Nancy and Charlotte, also teachers.

In the early seventies, there were only a few places to socialize: the bar, the Legion, two cafés, the bowling alley, and church. We had to make our own fun. On the weekends there were dances with local bands. We went *en masse* to the dances, which started about 11 p.m. and went on into the wee hours of the morning. We held dinner parties: some had themes and some were potluck. Everyone brought their best offerings and the results were amazing.

Living in an isolated setting awakened the desire to travel in some of us. In the mid-seventies, I headed off to Central America and Asia. I ran out of money while on the Philippines and made the decision to move to Hong Kong where I knew I could get work at the Bull and Bear Pub. In spite of working hard, I had a lot of fun there. It was good to live in a place where I was in the minority; it helped to reshape my thinking considerably. Travel also afforded me the opportunity to observe people from different cultures, how they behave and what they do with their lives. My curiosity about what makes me people tick was kindled and I still try to understand the intricate workings of the human mind.

Eventually I returned, and was rewarded by meeting the love of my life, Chris, who had just moved to Queen Charlotte to take the pharmacist position at the hospital. After a year of cautiously watching him from afar and getting to know him, we got together. One wintry night when we had a rare snow fall, he skied out to my cabin. The rest of this part of my story unfolds as it should when two people grow to love one another.

In my new life, I wanted to become even more self-sufficient. For a time, I tried animal husbandry. I wanted to start a garden and people advised me that the best way was to get piglets and let them do the plowing and fertilizing at the same time. The pigs, whom I called Pig and Pig, grew quickly on scraps from the hospital kitchen, supplemented by pig food. When it came time to slaughter them, I got help from my friends. As I had grown attached to them, we fortified ourselves with tequila. Unfortunately, the pigs sensed the danger and perhaps our level of intoxication; the event was a folly but the meat and the garden were a success. I tried once again to raise pigs on my friends' property. This time, the pigs escaped, ran across the street and started swimming out to an island in the inlet. We had to get a boat and head them back to shore. Needless to say this was my last attempt at animal husbandry.

The years came and went with work, parties, travel, friendships, and community involvement. If you want something to happen in a small town, you have to be a part of the process. In the early eighties I became involved with the Thrift Shop. It was started in 1972 to help support the tiny library by selling donated items at a low price. When the library moved to a permanent home in the new community centre, the local Women's Society took over the Thrift Shop. They operated the shop for a while and then my friend Nancy and I decided to volunteer. Clearly the shop needed new energy so we formed a non-profit society and threw ourselves into making the shop more viable. My involvement with the Thrift Shop lasted until I left the Charlottes in the fall of 2007. During that time we formed a board of directors, moved the Thrift Shop to a new location, renovated it several times, developed orientation, recruitment and management procedures, and steadily sought the help of volunteers. So many good people have given their time to keep it running. I understand that the Thrift Shop is still an important part of the community.

By 1985 I also became involved with providing housing for our senior citizens. At that time, when people were no longer able to live in their own homes, they had to leave the Islands. We needed other options as we were losing parts of our history and culture with the departure of our older residents. So I joined the board of the Queen Charlottes Heritage Housing Society. Planning had already begun for two independent-living seniors' apartment buildings, one in Masset and the other in Queen Charlotte. After construction was completed, the society split so that Masset could operate independently. Later we were able to obtain surplus federal housing and operate three homes for "those at risk of homelessness." We were also able to create an assisted-living facility.

Joline in Hong Kong, 1978.

My volunteer work with both of those societies was important to me and filled my need to give back to the community that had given me so much. I am grateful for those experiences and I take satisfaction and comfort in the role they continue to play in the community.

Over the years I worked at many jobs. I was an instructor for the community college, a social worker in child protection, and a mental health professional, to name a few. My last position was as a director for mental health and addictions with Northern Health, out of Terrace. I was fortunate to work with so many wonderful, dedicated people and so close to the Haida. I learned so much about generosity, and the importance of family and culture.

In the early nineties, my mother decided that she wanted to move to Canada to be closer to my brother and me. So a new chapter opened in my life: that of care-giver for my elderly parent. Eventually the time came for mother to give up her apartment. She moved into the hospital but, because she was still mobile, she had to move from there to a complex care facility. I made a promise to her to be there for the entire journey of her life, and both our destinies changed. My mother, with a little help from our home care nurse, was able to get into an excellent facility in Cumberland; Chris and I moved nearby.

The best-made plans are often transformed. My year on Haida Gwaii turned into 35. Throughout the years I have been fortunate to have deep and loyal friendships and rich experiences. Travel has been a constant part of my life, as has been community service. In my new community I am involved with the social issue of homelessness and dedicated to making a change for those who are in need. I remain in awe of the natural world. And when the wind blows, I frequently stand outside, with closed eyes, and return to my home on Haida Gwaii.

The Power of Community

by Lyn Pinkerton

IN AUGUST 1972, I came to Haida Gwaii from Boston via Prince Rupert. My partner, John, and I had stayed a while at Salt Lakes, learning to kayak. We had found a ride on a kind of fish boat that dropped us at Tow Hill near the northeast tip of Graham Island.

The first part of our paddle/sail down the east coast of Graham Island, favoured by westerlies, was idyllic. When we ran out of freshwater one day and landed, walking up to the first house we saw, we noticed a dulcimer hanging from the wall. When the owner learned that we had a dulcimer in our kayak, he invited us to stay. This improbable encounter became to start of a long friendship, the kind of friendships that happened easily on Haida Gwaii, and made me eventually think I would never leave.

I had dropped out of graduate school and was looking for something really different from the conservative anthropology department at Brandeis University outside of Boston, and also something different from the protected environment in which I was raised in Virginia. I wanted to define myself in a place where I was not identified by family or academic status. Both the southern lady and the ivory tower academic identities seemed unappealing and uninspired in this era of hope for major social change — change which had been in the air in the student movements in both the Boston area and in Paris where I had spent 1966-67. The civil rights movement, the anti-war movement, and finally the anarchist movement of Noam Chompsky, Howard Zinn, Murray Bookchin, and George

Woodcock: these people talked about the power of communities to govern themselves and solve a lot of their problems in ways far superior to central government solutions. They advocated a grassroots democracy in which people at the local level would have a lot more power to control their lives.

So in Kitimat, where we stopped off on the train trip across Canada, we heard about the exciting experiment on Hippie Hill in Queen Charlotte. People shared and helped each other and built interesting structures out of local materials. This was the place we wanted to end up after spending four months hunting and gathering from our kayak.

The first four months were what we originally came west for: to kayak the famous inland waterway. We then decided to go to the east coast of the Charlottes after a look at a map showing much lower rainfall there. Those four months were intensely memorable, our first adventure in learning to live off the land and sea as aboriginal people had done so brilliantly. We cut poles and pitched the tipi we had made for this trip in locations along the way where we camped for a week or more. We speared a deer from the kayak and lived on the dried meat, plus the pink and coho salmon runs, the huckleberries and, best of all, the low tide stews of octopus, mussels, urchins, chitons, limpits, periwinkle, and barnacles. During one period, other kayakers Dennis and Wendy joined us, as well as Dave, who read us portions of Swanton's *Haida Myths*, while we read Boas' 200 pages of fish recipes. We learned what a full-time job it was to live off the land, and that it must have taken a whole community to do it well.

One day when we were camped at Cumshewa, two Haida seine boats anchored and came ashore during low tide. We were hunting octopus and an elder on the boat showed us how to do it the traditional way, by bothering the octopus with a pointed stick until it finally came out of its lair. We were impressed by how gracious they were, especially given the fact that we had improperly camped on their reserve without asking permission. We had not foreseen that this Haida reserve would offer the only cleared area our tired bodies could find in the vicinity where a tipi could be easily pitched. Perhaps they forgave our clumsiness, as a week later we were kayaking up the inlet when the seiners, headed back to Prince Rupert, called us over and unloaded groceries into our kayaks, including the coveted canned butter. I still regret losing the notebook in which I recorded the names of the seiners, intending to return their kindness in the future. We weren't quite sure whether their gift was appreciation that we were living as they previously had, or charity to amateurs.

Arriving at Hippie Hill in November when it got too cold and windy for camping, Ken offered us the use of his father's cabin, and Ed offered us the use of his fish boat. We eventually became part of a vibrant and diverse community where people collected their firewood and built their water systems co-operatively. They had an accepting and tolerant attitude toward the eccentric newcomers who perhaps continued the tradition of First and Second World War draft resisters on the Charlottes who had wanted to be as far as possible from federal governments. Most impressive was the kindness of men toward the younger women, who wanted to learn bush skills and build their own cabins, which I eventually did after my partner and I separated. Many others helped too, so that everyone's cabin or project was a collective enterprise, based on a rough and uncalculated long-term exchange which resembled the generalized reciprocity of hunting and gathering societies around the world.

I became so fascinated by both the non-monetary exchange and the way the community fit into the logging and fishing industries that I decided it was worth finishing my Ph.D. by transferring to the sociology department and documenting it. That department was full of innovative and radical thinkers, so I was able to do "action research" a little before it became respectable. The best way to understand a system was to be part of the action!

The action against the logging industry in the seventies came initially from Islands Protection, a small group of counter-culture and young Haida activists advocating for the protection of south Moresby Island, where logging on steep slopes was causing substantial landslides and loss of fish and wildlife habitat. I respected this effort, but was more interested in the bigger question of how to have sustainable logging which allowed communities like the ones on the Charlottes to have long-term jobs which didn't hurt fish, wildlife, soils, and the whole forest ecosystem. In the Haida community next to Queen Charlotte, 80 per cent of the jobs were in the forest industry. Neither law nor policy required big industry to manage sustainably for communities in places like the Charlottes, so it was going to be up to us to bring this issue to public attention. Islands

Protection's activities made a big enough wave to label us one of a few hot spots in the province who got a Public Advisory Committee to the Forest Service, and I sat on this committee to raise the issue of sustainable logging and community stability. I wrote letters to the editor about these issues and was part of what became an island-wide movement for greater island-based control of resources.

Today South Moresby is protected and the Haida own what used to be part of MacMillan Bloedell's tree farm, and have a chance to gradually bring the massively over-cut forest back into a healthy one which can support future generations. Today Haida Fisheries has a chance to monitor the sport fisheries and apply pressure for sustainable commercial fisheries in the new marine protected area around South Moresby National Park. Today I sit on an advisory committee to that marine protected area and teach the social science of resource management at Simon Fraser University. I will be forever inspired by the wonderful chance a bunch of girls like us had to participate in the building of a social movement which pushed things on Haida Gwaii a bit closer to local control of local resources. Although we could not stop the industrial machine, we did help the next generation think of ways to do it better.

Living at Swan Bay

by Su-San Brown

I ARRIVED ON HAIDA GWAII in early September 1973. I had just finished working with my sister and her then-husband on a cougar study on Vancouver Island. Living in the bush was something I loved and thought I knew how to do.

Earlier I had squatted with a lot of other young people at Wreck Bay (Florencia Bay) in what is now Pacific Rim National Park. We were forced to leave when the park was created, and some of us chose to move farther out to the wilds of B.C. in the hope that we would be left undisturbed. I had fallen in love with living where the land meets the ocean, with building a house out of whatever I found washed up on shore, and with learning how to survive directly from what I could catch, grow, find or build with my own hands. Vancouver Island was becoming too populated for this, even though there was a history of it.

I am a fifth generation descendant of the first settlers in the Comox Valley, although I grew up an Air Force brat and lived all across Canada and England. When I was in Grade 5, we moved back to Vancouver Island and reconnected with my mother's family. My grandfather was an old man when I got to know him, but for most of his working life he had worked in the bush as a timber cruiser. I believe he loved just being in the old-growth forest – not cutting it down. In 1928, he travelled to Haida Gwaii to cruise timber and fell in love with the place. My grandmother had lived on Vancouver Island all her life, as had her mother before her, and would not even consider moving so far north, but the stories of the place persisted in our family, and we had a saying that if you had nowhere left to go, go to the Charlottes. So I did.

I didn't really know anyone when I moved here. I had one cedar box that I had built, a backpack, and my dog Sam. It didn't take long for me to find my way to the doorstep of Agate Annie, who was then living at the gap close to the mouth of the Tlell River. I was back with my own people, bush hippies squatting on the most beautiful land in the world. Once again it was not long before the powers that be decided to create a park there, and we were all forced to move again. I wanted to build a boat so I could travel with my house around me, and I wanted to do it in a place far enough away to not be disturbed for a while. Living in a cabin on the Mayer River, a few miles up the beach from Rick and Agate's cabin, was a young man from Texas who agreed to move into the remoteness of South Moresby Island and build a boat with me. I had money from working with my sister, so we bought tools, did a food order, and found a fisherman to take us down there and drop us off in early 1974.

There had been others who had gone before us, so we actually moved into a small cabin that had been left empty. We immediately started building a shed big enough for a boat with some plywood, poles and plastic. We milled the wood for the boat from logs we found on the beach, using an Alaska sawmill, a frame that clamps onto a chainsaw bar. The plans came from a book and the knowledge to even start the process came from Howard Chapelle's book *Boatbuilding*. This became our bible and we

The cabin at Swan Bay.

spent hours poring over it trying to understand exactly what he meant. The plans were drafted directly onto the floor of the boatshed and had to be redrawn many times when they faded from too much foot traffic. As our cabin was a 12-foot circle, most of our time was spent in the boatshed or outside.

I remember the first few months of being at Swan

Bay, how lonely I felt, rowing out in our skiff to try and jig a fish and weeping because I couldn't leave. It was just too far to row into town. Soon though, we settled into a routine of beachcombing, building, gardening and survival, and people started to arrive. Friends visited, tourists showed up; we even had neighbours for some years. One winter the population between Burnaby Narrows and Swan Bay was 11, the most we ever had. We had thought it would take a couple of years to build a boat; it took eight. But what an amazing place to do it. I feel blessed that I had the opportunity to experience living so isolated yet so included in the lives of the Haida, who still use South Moresby as their backyard and a source of physical and spiritual food.

One fall, some Haida friends picked us up at Swan Bay and took us to Hot Spring Island. It must have been around Thanksgiving because there was much discussion about how to cook the turkey. I jokingly asked, "didn't the Haida used to cook in pits with hot rocks and seaweed?" I then found myself in charge of preparing the bird. With lots of help we dug a pit, built a huge fire to heat the rocks, and layered it with seaweed. I did wrap the bird in tinfoil so we didn't have to eat more sand than necessary, and then we buried the whole thing to be uncovered at suppertime. It was perfect, or so my memory tells me.

We lived by a different time sense down there. Days of the week meant nothing, but seasons were all-important. We had no electricity, therefore not a lot of light other than daylight. Every hour of light was used to its fullest, even in the summer, a high energy time when we only got three or four hours of darkness. In the winter we slept and ate a lot, and told stories and played games and did small stuff that we could do by candlelight when darkness fell. When the tides were lowest in winter, it was always dark, but we went out anyway to gather abalone and scallops by candlelight and play with the phosphorescence in the water. Darkness holds no fear for me now.

I grew up at Swan Bay. I learned to trust myself and those around me. I learned to live a dream and that it is not always easy but so fulfilling to start and complete a big project. I also learned that ignorance is bliss, not knowing how hard the work was going to be until I was so far in that walking away was not an option. And that "the teacher will come when the student is ready." So many times we found ourselves at a difficult point in the boatbuilding process and someone would arrive on our beach with the knowledge of how to continue, or at least with a pair of helping hands. Our boat was a testament of patience, hard work, and our willingness to step off the cliff and believe that the wings would appear and we would learn to fly.

The *Swan Bay*, as we named our boat, still floats. She is owned and sailed by a young man who is curious about the story of how she came to be built. Maybe someday I will tell him how we launched her on March 8, 1982, and finally sailed her to town, our only power sails and a sculling oar. How our approach to the dock was a bit too fast. How Paul, a solidly-built Haida man, calmly said, "throw me the rope." He braced himself and stopped our forward momentum as if we had tied ourselves to a tree.

I left the boat and the life I had been living in the wilds of South Moresby. The area would be protected by the creation of Gwaii Haanas National Park. For the first time, I was in total agreement that this was the only way to save that place from the greed of humankind. I had seen first-hand the devastation to the herring and abalone stocks in an area that had once sustained us. At least the trees would be left and hopefully the ocean will be able to repair herself. I left because I wanted more human contact and the inspiration I get from that. But I didn't go far. I settled in Tlell, where I raised my daughter and created an extended family of my own.

The boat named the Swan Bay.

Haida Gwaii is my home and has been for 40 years. I have watched people come and go and have dear friends who do not live here but still hold it in their hearts. This place is special. There is a wilderness that I need. A silence and a darkness that I need.

I hope that mine is not the last generation that will search for a chance to live a dream even though it goes against normal standards of an appropriate way to live.

At the Edge of the World

by Karen McKinster

IN THE SPRING OF 1973 I was working as a nurse's aide in an old folks' home outside of Denver, Colorado. I really liked the old folks and I had decided to go to nursing school in the fall. A mutual friend introduced me to a nice young man from Canada who had come for a visit. By the time he returned to the Queen Charlotte Islands, he'd invited me to come spend the winter with him there, but I was going to nursing school, so I regretfully declined. Then in late July, the hospital that sponsored the school wrote to say they wouldn't be having classes that fall because they were renovating. They refunded the deposit I'd sent in – $50 I think it was. That was enough money for five fill-ups for my old V.W. bus, and so, at loose ends, I decided to head north.

I remember that I had just shy of $300 when I set out. I hadn't even seen the Queen Charlotte Islands on a map – the legend had always covered them – but I had faith that if I got to Prince Rupert, my next step would become apparent. Once I got to Prince Rupert I found I needed to get on the *Northland Prince*, my first exposure to ocean travel. The boat was 329 feet long and provided freight and passenger service to several northern communities for up to 120 passengers. It was a classy way to go. Once I recovered from seeing my bus containing my belongings – and my cat and my dog, McTavish – hoisted from the dock head and, rocking gently, lowered into the hold, I could relax and enjoy the trip. There were white tablecloths and actual waiters. I thought this was normal. There might have been flowers on the table, or maybe I've made that up in the intervening years. I don't have any recollection of my accommodations on the voyage. (I was also lucky enough to be on the last sailing of the *Northland Prince*, in October 1976, from Queen Charlotte City to Vancouver.)

Once I arrived in Masset and met my friend, we went home. He was living on North Beach, a couple of miles past Tow Hill, about 25 miles east of Masset. The beach was wild and gorgeous, virtually devoid of people and vehicles. He had resurrected an old settler's log cabin, the Baker cabin everyone called it, and it was both more and less than I had imagined. Primitive and glorious. I'd rarely been to any beach in my life, always with the expectation of bikinis and sunburn. On North Beach, not so much. The wind was constant, in rain or sun, and even in August I was glad of my old Irish fisherman's sweater.

It didn't take long to discover that D and I weren't suited and I was totally out of my depth. That was when I met Judy. She and her beautiful two-year-old daughter T'ai Li were staying temporarily with Jenny just a few miles down the road toward Masset. She was working on completing a treehouse she had discovered while kayaking one day on the Kumdis River, a couple of kilometres outside of Port Clements. Judy was, and is, a consummate bush woman. She could do anything. She never ceased to amaze me and I learned a lot from her. She did it all: dyeing and spinning wool, dressing out a deer, gathering mushrooms, catching fish with a piece of perlon and a hook. The basic framework of the treehouse was bolted to four spruce trees about 10 feet off the ground. It was about eight-by-ten feet with a sleeping loft and, eventually, an airtight stove. Anyway, she invited me to join them.

We got moved in sometime prior to New Year's 1974. I don't think

The treehouse on the Kumdis River

Judy actually unpacked anything, as she moved out almost immediately to start a life with a fellow we'd recently met. So I was alone for a few weeks. Sometimes late at night, if I'd remembered to get fresh batteries, I'd listen to a radio station out of Seattle or San Francisco. They seemed so much farther away than the miles would indicate. I completely lost touch with the music scene that had played such an important part in my life up until that time.

One day, there was a knock at the door and there stood Dorothy, Judy's friend, who had come to stay. Judy had forgotten to mention to me that Dorothy would

Karen & McTavish, 1974.

be coming. So I consolidated my stuff to make room for her and her dog. As you might imagine, it was close quarters, but we were nothing if not adaptable. She got the loft, so I had to give up my sewing room, and I got the main floor. Fortunately, I'd just completed the down sleeping bag kit I was putting together with the use of an old hand-crank sewing machine I'd borrowed.

So there we were, me and McTavish and Dorothy and Stroodle. Some-where along the line we acquired a couple of kittens, Joba and Sienna. The Kumdis River was spitting distance away, but as it was tidal we had to pack freshwater for drinking and bathing from a creek a short distance away. I learned to bathe in a minute amount of water, but washing all that hair required a bit more effort. I don't remember much about acquiring firewood. Occasionally, a manly man with a chainsaw would happen by and buck up a few logs for us. There was always sufficient wood for our needs. Also, every couple of weeks an old fellow from Port Clements would come up the river on the tide in his little tugboat and split us a week's worth of firewood. Then, depending on the tide, he'd stay for a cup of tea or motor away before the boat got stranded. I think he was checking to see that we were okay, and it was an excuse to get out in his boat.

I don't recall ever having a cross word with Dorothy. We were both busy and able to entertain ourselves. The animals worked out their place in the hierarchy. We didn't spend a whole lot of time indoors except to sleep and eat. We cohabited there until about April, when we migrated to Port Clements to look for work.

During this period there were parties and potlucks and dances, much to-ing and fro-ing between North Beach, Masset, Port Clements, Tlell, and Queen Charlotte City. I had more interaction with the north end of the island, and it was then that I decided I'd never be quite cool enough for Charlotte.

I was so taken with the lifestyle of the Islands. It was like stepping back in time. I had grown up on a farm in Kentucky, but moved to a more urban centre, then to Atlanta: I'd become a city girl, at least on the surface. Life on the Charlottes was, on the one hand, hard: keeping the woodstove fed, packing buckets of water, canoeing down the Kumdis River home to the treehouse after a trip to town or, if the tide was out, walking 40 minutes. But it was easy, too. There was an abundance of food, razor clams, deer, crab, and a variety of mushrooms. There always seemed to be bits of work to keep some cash happening. Food was an important commodity, as it is anywhere, I guess. For the items that we didn't hunt and gather, there were "food orders."

What a treat those were. I'd never experienced the like. Groups would gather, hunched over catalogues, and place orders for grains, dried fruit, honey, cooking oils, all sorts of food, plain and exotic. One household could share a case of something with another, or could keep it all for themselves. The more you ordered, the less the freight would cost. You could combine with another group if the timing worked out. Somebody would phone the order in to the wholesaler and, a couple of weeks later, it would miraculously appear. Then some of the group would convene and sort and divide the loot, and everybody would be thrilled with their purchases, or disappointed the dried apricots didn't come, or pissed off that the long-grain rice had been sent instead of the short-grain that had been ordered. Again. The bookkeeping nightmare followed: the cheques would be collected and submitted, nobody would starve, and we all looked forward to what we'd order next time.

One particularly memorable food order brought us a 30-pound bucket of honey. T'ai Li was so excited she got a spoon and just dug into that bucket. She was covered with honey from her gorgeous curly hair down to the ground. And the kitten Joba too; they both got baths in the galvanized tub by the oil stove. I loved food order time, and I still do.

There were a few established couples, many with a kid or two. There were a few of us single women and a multitude of single men. Couples would hook up for a few weeks or months, then they'd break up, casually or with drama, then after a respectful mourning period, some guy would come sniffing around to see if maybe he could make the cut. One of the courtship rituals that always tickled me was that you could identify a serious suitor if he showed his devotion by digging a new outhouse hole. This conferred a certain level of commitment.

Everybody, it seemed to me, was very capable, and most were determined to be as self-sufficient as possible. People were learning to garden, or learning to adapt what they knew of gardening to the not-always-friendly climate. There was talk of being ready "when the crunch comes" to take care of ourselves. It was the first place I'd ever lived where people – mostly women – not only baked bread, but also ground the wheat; they not only knitted socks and toques and sweaters, but they also carded, dyed and spun the wool. We picked and dried mint and roseships, saved onion skins and marigolds for dyeing, collected shaggy mane and chanterelle mushrooms; we canned salmon and deer meat, and dried seaweed. We learned how to innovate and make do.

I would write my mother back in Tennessee, or sometimes phone her and tell her of my adventures. I can just see her sitting there, shaking her head as she heard how I was embracing canning food and packing water and splitting firewood – things she'd worked long and hard to leave behind. I believe she came to understand that it makes a difference if you choose the lifestyle rather than doing those things because you have no options.

There were a number of ways to earn a living. There were teachers and nurses and social workers, pretty standard fare. Some guys were carpenters or carpenter wannabes, learning by trial and error with varying degrees of success. Some made their living tree-planting in the summer months, mostly on the mainland. Some became fishermen, some loggers. There were a few with moneyed families who were dabbling at subsistence living, but I didn't know about them until much later, because everybody lived at pretty much the same level. There was a memorable L.I.P. (Local Initiative Project) grant where a bunch of hippies were hired to build a shelter over an abandoned cedar canoe that had been uncovered during a logging operation. Coffee breaks were memorable for the s'mores that were concocted. I heard later that the shelter had fallen down, but the canoe was still there.

When I left the Charlottes nearly a year after my arrival, I looked for a similar subculture and came fairly close to finding one in the mountains of North Carolina, but the pull of the north was strong. I returned a couple of times in the late seventies, renewing friendships and keeping the connection alive. I knew I wasn't meant to work a regular job. It seems so obvious now, but at the time I kept trying to slot into "normal." I wanted to do physical work, grow food, have animals, be self-sufficient – but I couldn't figure out how or where I could make a living at it. When I returned to Queen Charlotte City in 1980 to reconnect with friends, I met Dave, who would become my husband. He is a fisherman, and I became one too – doing physical work, definitely not a 9-to-5 job. We bought property in Dodge Cove in 1984. I've been able to do some gardening, and we've caught lots of fish and hunted deer – so we've been somewhat self-sufficient. We raised our daughter Claire on the boat, fishing every summer. She's launched now, and we're planning to spend more time back on Haida Gwaii, reconnecting with old and new members of our tribe. I have maintained contact with a number of the women I knew from my first trip north, and have of course met new ones. It's always interesting to compare notes with friends who were on Haida Gwaii when I first came. We knew the same people, we were sometimes at the same events. How could we possibly not have met until 15 or 20 years later?

When I was first first approached to write for this book, I was asked what brought me north to this place of incredible ruggedness and beauty. I thought about the women I knew then and now, and the stories of our adventures. I thought that many of the stories might be fairly short: hormones. And that is true, but it is only a partial truth. A more complete answer includes the sense of community we created and the growth we achieved as we became full-fledged grown-ups. The dreams we were pursuing stayed constant or fell by the wayside and were replaced by other dreams. Families were created, and many of those kids have a strong connection to this amazing landscape. I like to think that Haida Gwaii will be important in Claire's life, as it has been in mine.

For Dan

by Agate Annie VerSteeg

A LOT HAD HAPPENED in the seven years since I had moved to the Char-lottes, but nothing quite like this. This was new and uncharted territory for me. Of course it involved a man. A sweet guy named Dan, who was working his way into my ever-fragile heart. I was not a person who knew much about boundaries when it came to affairs of the heart. I tended to throw myself and everything I owned madly, passionately and completely into these things, but these were the seventies and we were learning to be liberated women. We were not supposed to feel tied down or beholden to any one person. For a romantic like me, this was a very difficult situation. That the story ended prematurely, because Dan died suddenly, changed everything.

I had first heard about the Charlottes in 1972 from a friend of a friend. He was returning from his first trip to the northwest and travelling back to Park City, Utah to work at his winter job. I was going to Idaho State University in Pocatello, Idaho. He told these wonderful romantic tales of life in the bush. Basically, how people were moving there and living off the land. They were catching and canning salmon, cultivating and harvesting gardens, and getting higher than kites on the local organic psilocybin mushrooms. They were making it by financially on very little, and worked on government grants for the Department of Fisheries dur-ing the peak seasons. It all sounded incredible to me. I think I fell in love with the Charlottes right then and there, although it would be about nine months before I saw him again and 11 months before we headed to the

Charlottes. By that time, I had spent so much time romanticizing about my new life in the bush! Reality and fantasy are rarely the same.

I was a southern California girl, born in 1952 to an upper middle class family: Mom, Dad, my sister Betsy, and me. We lived in San Marino, went to private schools, had a nice house, live-in help and a 58-foot boat moored at the L.A. Yacht Club. We shared the boat with our grandparents; I am pretty sure they owned and paid the upkeep on her and we got to enjoy her on weekends sailing to Catalina Island. All of our parents' friends had boats and they'd all sail over on the weekends too. It was pretty much a party scene for the parents and a free-for-all for the kids. We loved it. We'd swim and row our dinghys around the cove where all the boats were moored, we'd look for wild boar on shore and check for moray eels during low tides. It seemed like everybody was happy there. My parents got along, they laughed, relaxed and enjoyed themselves. This may have had something to do with the fact that just about every boat there had a paid deckhand onboard so the responsibilities the adults had were minimum. I learned my love for the out-of-doors in Catalina.

My mom was a smart and savvy woman. It could not have been easy to be a woman in those days; it's no wonder cocktail hour had replaced quilting bees in the suburbs. She had the good sense to send me off to a month-long farm camp every summer. At the camp they bred all the cows, goats, horses, pigs, chickens and ducks to have their offspring during summer so we could experience a real working farm. From birth to slaughter, we saw it all. The counsellors were young and very hip. They brought their babies and toddlers with them. They breastfed their babies everywhere, the animals gave birth everywhere, and I was fascinated by it all! All that new life, all that feeding of their young. I was enthralled by pregnancy, birth and post-partum choices.

I arrived on the Charlottes in the fall of 1973. I was up for an adventure and I had brand new copies of *Our Bodies, Ourselves* and *Spiritual Midwifery*. I was ready for women's lib, romance, home birth, and living in the bush. We built our first little cabin on the Tlell River. It was sweet. I learned how to tell one kind of log from another while beachcombing for building materials. I split cedar shakes with a froe and mallet. Joannie and Suzie taught me how to split rounds of wood with a sledge hammer and wedge, chop wood with a big double bit axe, how to split cedar into kindling with a hatchet, and make a great fire in a wood heater or wood cook stove. This was an invaluable lesson, a basic and important life skill in the bush and my first step towards independence. I will be forever grateful to those two lovely women.

People were talking about having their babies at home, in their cabins. I had been to many births while living in Idaho and working in a small 28-bed hospital. I had received great training from some kind and loving natural birth doctors. I thought the least I could do was offer my help in case people wanted some assistance. I was fortunate to attend quite a few births on the Charlottes, amazing powerful women having their babies in their own beds with their partners helping. My wonderful assistant, Jane, gave me courage and strength. She went on to become a registered nurse and I attended a school for midwifery. It was an honor and a privilege to assist the couples on the Charlottes, who trusted me to help them bring their babies into this world.

The Parks Department of Canada decided in 1975 that squatting was forbidden and we had to move. We built an amazing 14-by-30-foot houseboat. She was a beauty. We cut every piece of wood with an Alaska sawmill, split all the shakes for the roof, hand caulked every seam of the hull, hand planed the wood for the interior and moved it to the head of Cumshewa Inlet where we were gonna live happily ever after. Wrong! We split up, sold the houseboat, and I moved back to the Tlell River where I bought a sweet little cabin just about half a mile from the end of the road. I was on my own. I had a chainsaw, axes, hammer, hatchet, shovels, kerosene lamps, a sewing machine, some money left over from the sale of the houseboat, and my trusty dog, Sadie. I felt incredibly empowered and weak at the same time. I had been there for about a year when I started falling for Dan.

The houseboat.

He was tall and handsome and bearded. His hair was strawberry blonde, his eyes were blue, and he was and was, by far, one of the kindest men I had and have ever met. There was a fatal flaw though: he really liked me. I was of the mindset that if a man really liked me, he must be screwed up because who could ever like me just for being who I am? It seemed wrong! Plus, he was a logger; he was working for a logging company who was cutting down the trees we were trying to save.

He loved coming down to the cabin and hanging out. He wanted to sharpen my saw and buck up the logs for winter wood. He was willing to turn the garden, help can the salmon, drink a beer, smoke a joint, and make amazing love to me while Joan Armatrading sang softly in the background on the cassette player. He was the whole package.

We went everywhere together, parties in Tlell, dances in Skidegate, the pub in Port Clements, grocery shopping in Queen Charlotte City, and long walks on the beach. Dan helped me get my groceries and kerosene from the end of the road down the river to my cabin. He helped me paddle the canoe, or drag it, depending on which way the tide was going. He'd haul as much as I'd let him. He'd admonish me (sweetly) for running the saw in my flip flops without headphones, or for chopping wood in shorts. I was in love but afraid to admit it, afraid my feelings for this sweet and handsome man meant I wasn't independent. I wasn't a woman's libber; I was letting society down.

One night we were at a party at a friend's house in Tlell. People were playing music, kids were running around, the food was fabulous. The food on the Charlottes was *always* fabulous. One of the guests had recently had a baby, whose birth I had attended about six weeks before. I was sitting in a big overstuffed chair, holding this precious baby girl in my arms when Dan walked over and sat beside me. We both just drank in the newness

Annie's cabin on the Tlell River.

of this little baby girl. Dan looked at me and said, "you know, Agate, we could do this, this could be our baby, our life." I was dumbstruck. Because when you peeled away all the layers of independence and liberation in me, you'd find a young woman who'd been waiting all her life to hear those words. At that moment I realized that all I really wanted was to be a wife and mother.

So what did I do? Did I get honest and speak what was in my heart, fall into his arms and tell Dan how much his words meant to me? No, silly, these were the seventies. I smiled and just sort of dropped the subject. I was scared. Within a couple of weeks I told Dan that I thought we should see other people. I knew one of our friends really liked him and it'd be okay with me if he spent time with her. I even tried to believe it was okay. I rekindled an old romance with a jerk who, of course, made me feel right at home. Dan was against the whole idea of us seeing other people, but if it made me happy, he'd come around less and try seeing other people. He moved most of his belongings out of my cabin. I pushed him away.

Annie in her cabin.

It was coming on summer after another long and dark winter. The winter days are short, the winter nights incredibly long and oft times filled with spectacular northern lights. I wanted some sun, I needed time to think things through, I needed time to talk myself out of falling for a man who had fallen for me. I decided to go see my mom in La Jolla, California, a beautiful town just north of San Diego. Dan was happy to cabin-sit for me while I was gone. He loved my dog Sadie too and took great care of her. We had still been seeing each other and enjoying each other's company. We'd have a great time and great sex, but I was still scared and still really stupid.

I spent a month in La Jolla. It was beautiful. The sun was warm, the ocean water was warm and clear. Being in the constant sunshine and warmth felt so good! Hot running water and flush toilets were fabulous. The crowds and traffic were bothersome, but feeling all that sun was so amazing. It made me think about moving. There was a part of me that felt like I was home; I am, after all is said and done, a California girl. Maybe go to school and become a licensed midwife to fulfill that dream? But what about Dan? What should I do? I had lots of unfinished business up north and was in no way prepared not to go back, but the seed of moving had been planted. I was already looking into schools and formulating a plan.

I returned to the Charlottes and to Dan and Sadie. It was really good to see both of them. We had some fun times. Dan was working on going out to a hand-logging claim on the west coast; he'd be gone for awhile. I had found a midwifery school in El Paso, Texas but I needed to learn Spanish first. Dan's hand-logging claim would take about six months to complete, and my schooling would take over a year. We didn't make any sort of commitment to each other but we didn't say good-bye either. Sadie and I headed south. I was living at my mom's with plans to go to Guatemala for a two-month Spanish immersion program before starting school in El Paso. Everything was coming together. I was achieving a goal. I had a man who cared for me (with no commitment, of course) and I was feeling good about life.

Dan headed out to the west coast to set up the hand-logging claim. He was on a tugboat called the *Detour* with the woman he shared the claim with. They made it through Skidegate Narrows and were headed north when they struck a rock, or somehow started to take on water. Tugboats sink fast. Very fast. They were both trapped in the wheelhouse. Neither one made it out.

I was in total shock. I was sad and lost and heartbroken. I returned to the Charlottes, sold the cabin, its contents, gathered up what was left of my belongings and left the beautiful and moody Tlell River for good. Retrospectively, I started running.

That was just over 30 years ago. Sometimes in life, we have no choice but to move on. I learned Spanish, I went to school, moved back to La Jolla and delivered babies. I married, had two children, divorced, and survived another broken heart. Living on or by the Pacific Ocean is a sort of sanctuary. The sea is soothing and constantly changing. It is my home.

Dan's still down there, somewhere on the bottom, too deep for recovery.

Finding Home

by Dorothy Garrett

PEOPLE I KNEW MOVED TO the Charlottes before me. Some from the communal house on Gillette Street in Prince George where I lived for a time, came and moved on. Others, like my forever friend Judy, came and stayed.

I chose a different path, seeking adventure, keen to explore the world. In 1972 I embarked on my first big trip: hitchhiking to Montreal and flying to Bermuda, Antigua, Barbados and Grenada. When my travelling companion decided to stay in Trinidad, I carried on alone to Guyana, Surinam, Brazil, Uruguay, Argentina, Chile and Peru. As a blissfully ignorant 18 year-old female travelling alone, I learned the world can be dangerous and sometimes lonely. In Chile during the chaos of the coup, with local help I managed to leave unscathed. Desperate refugees spilled into Peru where I was naïve enough to lend most of my money to a young Chilean family and have my passport stolen. Unable to continue with a temporary passport, after eight months of travel, I returned to Canada in 1973 to regroup.

I wrote in my notebook words that resonated:

> Young was I once and wandered alone
> And naught of the road I knew
> Rich did I feel when a comrade I found
> For a man is a man's delight.
>> ~excerpt from "Hávamál" in *The Poetic Edda*

I remained transient, sometimes living in my camperized 1953 Mercury Panel. I wanted to experience more about people, ideas, places and cultures so different from what I grew up with in Prince George. Making and keeping connections with friends and family kept me grounded. I wrote letters, lots of them. And after my parents both passed, my letters came back to me. My parents had saved every one.

I carried with me a strong sense of my own culture, the culture of my generation, of female independence, of knowing I could do whatever I set my mind to, and of living simply with a smaller footprint, close to nature. In those days, I had a sense of being part of something bigger than myself. When I left home at 16, after an initial fascination with the big city, I found I felt my best when I was close to nature. The city began to represent alienation, conspicuous consumption, a trap. I wanted out. I worried about the unhealthy food I was eating. I worried about environmental degradation and the garbage we create. I wanted to do things differently. Still, I didn't move to the Queen Charlotte Islands with a particular intention, with a plan or expectations. I was working wherever I could find work, putting a little aside, and dreaming about the next big trip. The Charlottes were where I wanted to be at the time.

I'd never been to the Charlottes. The directions were vague. Something about tides and rivers and finding the way after there were no roads or trails. I didn't know much. I knew I wasn't to bring many belongings. Judy specifically told me not to bring many clothes because there wouldn't be room for them inside. While I wondered what that really meant, what I did know was my best friend was there. Things would work out. I left my vehicle with my parents, packed a few boxes and my dog Stroodle and boarded the *Northland Prince*. Judy and her two year-old daughter T'ai Li picked us up in a borrowed car. Rushing before the tide went out and the river became too shallow to navigate, we drove straight to the Kumdis River and loaded food, gear, my boxes, ourselves, and the dog into a canoe. Darkness fell as we paddled. Shadows appeared. In the twilight I saw bears around every corner. Occasionally, I'd say, "Is that a bear?"

"No, it's just a log," came the response.

"Are you sure?" For all my worldliness I was, after all, a city chick.

The treehouse wasn't quite finished. It was built on a large platform between the tops of four trees, with a small surrounding deck and a little wood stove for heating and cooking. Karen, who'd arrived earlier, Judy and I handsawed the last finishing touches. We cut and split firewood laboriously. For a while Judy, T'ai Li, Karen, her dog McTavish, her two cats, myself, and my dog Stroodle all lived together in the treehouse until Judy moved to North Beach to fix up another cabin. Judy later

On the way to the treehouse on the Kumdis River.

bore her second child on her own in Jenny's cabin. Life leisurely focused on survival. It took time but there was no sense of urgency. The land and sea provided. Much of what we did centered around food: gathering, preserving, preparing, sharing. From one of my letters, March 10, 1974: "Yesterday Jude & me and Dutes canned a great garbage pail full of cockles and razor clams & horse clams & scallops. I know now how to clean them & can them & cook them...I'd like to learn about seaweed too and how to dry kelp. It's suppose to be really good for you." I kept a notebook with recipes I wanted to remember like super cosmic salad, wheat germ muffins, pumpkin soup, and banana nut bread. I recorded all the wild edible plants, where to find them, and how to use them. Other things we did more for the pleasure of doing and sense of accomplishment rather than out of dire necessity. One entry read: "I've started making candles again since now we use them for a reason rather than just on special occasions like you do when you've got electricity. Learned how to make dip ones & drip ones & ones from balloons. I really enjoy dipping them." Judy and I worked together to tease, card and spin fleece, dye the wool with natural dyes, and learned to weave, knit or crochet sweaters, jackets, hats and socks. David helped sell my macramé in the hotel gift shop. We'd occasionally paddle or walk into town for supplies, for a shower, or to socialize. Although having a real shower in the Karlscourt Hotel in Masset was a special treat, I didn't particularly miss having running water, power, tiled floors, or flush toilets I'd taken for granted all my life. I learned I could live without them. I learned to appreciate the little things in my life and I learned to be grateful. I loved it.

Karen and I spent the winter living in the treehouse, but in the spring of 1974 the need to earn money drove us into town. I found a job in Port Clements until June with Human Resources at $3 an hour. Fully intending to return to our retreat in the woods on April 8, I wrote my mom: "Bought a shovel yesterday and next weekend we're going to start digging the out house and well at the tree house. Then we can start on the garden, filling in the ditches, a smoke house, and if there's any energy left, a sauna bath. The guy that owns the property brought us some glass for the windows and is going to help dig the well. He said that we could live there as long as we like. Really a nice person." But the day after Easter I wrote: "This weekend Karen and I and a couple of other people went out to the tree house. We got the holes for the outhouse and well dug but it was very half-hearted as when we got there we discovered, to our horror, someone had sawed our trees down. They left the tree house standing but cut the trees just above the platform, one smashed the main supports to the ramp when it fell. The buck-saw was broken too. We cried. The guy who owns the land offered to help us build another back in the woods a bit where we won't be seen. But I dunno, we haven't decided yet what to do."

June 9, 1974: "Last weekend someone went out and burned our house to the ground. I had a dream during winter of the tree house burning

Dorothy at the door of Jenny's North Beach cabin.

and the trees on fire. I didn't pay much attention to it at the time. They burned a building about a half mile from us too. The decision's been made for us whether we'll return there to live." It no longer felt like a safe place to be.

I lived in Jenny's cabin on North Beach while she was away. Stroodle and I beachcombed every day, gathering treasures for projects. I loved the solitude, the freedom and independence but every once in a while, I'd walk the 26 kilometres to town to check the mail, and perhaps run into a certain person I was interested in. Instead of isolation, I felt a sense of community.

I wrote to my parents: "Had a fine day yesterday. Went to a big picnic in Tlell, ate and played baseball and played guitars. A lot of people and dogs and kids and a good time by all." The Charlottes captured my heart. I'd found my comrades. I wanted to build a house.

Work was sporadic, short term with minimal pay. Six hours lying on the floor of a fish boat on the way to North Island, throwing up while waves crashed over my head, squelched any fantasy I had of making money as a deckhand. And there was still a lot of world to see. Over the next four years I came and went several times. Finding work on the Islands eluded me so I worked on the mainland. I travelled to Europe, Turkey, Afghanistan, India and Nepal. But when I thought of home, I thought of the Charlottes. It was home base. On one of my mainland sojourns, I got married. I travelled to Guatemala, Ecuador, Panama, Costa Rica, Belize and Mexico with husband number one and divorced shortly after. I still wanted to build a house on the Charlottes. This time, I planned my move. I took a log building course in the winter at the college in Prince George. I enrolled in college in Vancouver for the fall session to improve my job opportunities so I could stay on-island to work. While I was tree planting that summer, earning money for college, I met my life partner. Immediately following my graduation, in 1979, I returned with Mike on the inauguration sailing of the *Queen of the North* to Prince Rupert. We sent the truck on Riv Tow's barge and arrived by float plane in Masset.

This time, finding work came easy. Within a few days I was building a prototype log house in Tlell with Axel and with Jai, who was hoping to start a log house building company. Finding a place to live was a whole lot harder. We started off by house-sitting for Lea and Bob in Queen Charlotte while they were out fishing. As their return date drew nearer, in desperation, we'd knock on doors inquiring about any empty buildings we saw, no matter how dilapidated, offering to work on them. At the last second Lyn Pinkerton interviewed us to rent her little house on Hippie Hill. We had passive solar heat, a 45-gallon drum woodstove, a rain barrel and outhouse, we showered on a stump beside the house. It was perfect. We settled in Queen Charlotte City and Mike and I have been building ever since. We have a room in our guest house overlooking the water that we named "The Kumdis Room," in honour of the treehouse, a special place in a special time.

From the Lighthouse

by Dory Spencer

1973. VANCOUVER-TOFINO, BEACH SQUATTING, dripping plastic shelters, $10 rusting wood stoves, eating limpets and clams. Live in Simon Fraser Housing Co-op, become vegetarian, Rolling Stones party, 17th birthday box of joints. Crisis Centre training, high school dropout. Hitchhike Canada, everyone goes to Europe, I'm to Grade 12.

Teach night school pottery, model for art schools. Meet Skid, Qualicum Beach tenting, sand dollar mobiles. Prepare to move north, coast guard job, survival on isolated island in the middle of the coast.

Sent to Prince Rupert, overnight, Rupert Hotel burned down. Take the *Alexander Mackenzie* freighter down coast to Addenbrooke Island lightstation. Disappointing tower – a light bulb.

Lightkeeper Ray, really cool, tame deer in yard. Ruth, his wife, knits argyle socks, tells stories, and reads. All at the same time. Skiff into Rivers Inlet, float homes, long-gone canneries, dance halls underwater, see the jail bars in the low tide mud. Fish Egg Inlet, sugar shack, frozen over in winter, trappers skin otter, martin, throw carcasses on rocks, eagles flock.

Johnny, hand-logger, won't eat prawns, pulled body from bay, "the guy was covered in them." Ray, bowlegged hunting guide, bullet holes in his cabin walls. "Crazy New York clients, shooting guns. They couldn't handle a drink." Flipped his chopper in Glacier Lake, swam ashore dragging his friend, learned to fly a Piper. Jack, "Silver Grizzly," red cheeks, twinkle eyes, "there's an otter aboard, sleeping in my bunk."

Fishermen search for us, a really big blow, it came up too fast, we plowed into it for hours, I bailed, each wave higher than the other.

Topmast out my window, staysail and poles, last sailing-troller, quietly follows tideline. I bake bread, build gardens, cook, catch fish. Each room gets repainted, three times a year, endless days. The Lights are lonely, I wave at boats going by, lucky to get a visitor. Two Owekeeno guys appear out of nowhere. "Don't come near! We smell awful strong!" Offer us gifts, buckets of smoked, fermented and fresh oolichans.

Ron and Cecilia, ministers on *Thomas Crosby* United Church boat. She bites an apple, offers it to deer. The deer turns away. "Halitosis!" laughs Ray, winks his joke on her. He takes me jigging. "It's a shark!" I drop it in horror. He grabs the line, a dogfish, all's fine. Aims skiff at whale in middle of Fitz Hugh Sound. Stops. Where did it go? Silence all round. Sudden breath explodes, its rank smell descends, reach out to touch it. He laughs at my frightened face. "Welcome to the coast."

Months of silence. Sound carries far over the water. Sixth sense knows before it happens. Something will show up, tension in air. Energy vibrates.

Wind gusting strong. Window glass bends inward, out. Listen to radio. "Mayday! Five men in the water!" Searchlights, flash in the blackness, wild sea, storm rages on. Egg Island lighthouse, each rotation our lights touch, reaching across fishermen, pulling up the bodies. Early morning, radio calm, storms done, they've gone to anchor in Safety Cove, the herring fleet has just begun.

1977. Boat Bluff lightstation, even more insignificant light bulb tower. Seven-knot riptide is strong, deep water. Sharp turn in the channel, looming white prow cuts the view. Towering decks of a cruise ship, cameras ready at the rails. Sally's dress shop, deck four, has a sale, salon for your hair, cocktails by the pool. Early dawn light, two sasquatch hunters slip quietly by, camouflaged boats, camouflaged coats. Wolves sing up and down mountains, the ones we never see behind our house, answer back. Their howls are louder than the rest. A Bell chopper lands on the pad, "we're lost in this fog" says the pilot. Speedboats roar up with a road map, empty tanks needing gas. Coast guard Sikorsky helicopter lands once a month, brings mailbag, groceries, an awkward visit. Forgotten social graces, shyness settled in.

It's the way of the coast, gather food, dig it, can it, dry it, gift it, trade it. Put some milk in the clams, they spit out the sand. Salmon neck chowder, best part of the fish, good for your health. Which way is the tide? Firewood; fir or alder? How high is it floating? Wet or dry? Roar out in the skiff: dog it, tow it, chop it, pile it. Whales blow right beside the skiff. Buzz bombs on the rod, cast off the rocks, bring it in slow, easy now, up leaps the salmon, oh it's a fighter, jumping bejesus! Johnny caught a halibut, bigger than the skiff, shot it, trying to find the brain. But it just kept bucking, broke the gaff right in half. Once a tree fell on his head, almost dead, raced the skiff for his mom, size of an egg the lump on his head, went home with fresh bread. We're on his boat, out with a log tow, out comes the rifle, he shot at the seal, "didn't aim to kill just to scare, teach it a lesson — not wise to get curious." City guy, came up for work. Which way did he go, where is he now, it's been hours, call out a search party, must have got lost. You check the sugar shack down Fish Egg, I'll go the other way, call out the big guys, in comes a Buffalo, flight passes all day. Sparky's found safe in the bay, a couple nights away. There's a blow to the south, coming towards us, must be a Grey. Look, it's blowing blood, behind it, beside it, slice fins of the Killers. Blubber chunk on the beach, floats in with the tide. Bull Harbour radio, barely awake, report 4:40 weathers, three times a day, never to meet, only by voices, alpha-bravo-charlie. They gave me my name "Dory."

Rupert connections travel by, Richard stops, plays kazoos, Alan's new boat slips anchor. Bill and Wendy teach me to drop-spin raw wool, with a chopstick and apple. Peter, old Dutch carpenter, builds concrete helicopter pads, drinks gin with sugar. Ian, relief keeper, they become longtime friends.

We leave once a year, go into Rupert, Savoy for beer. Ring the bell, a round for all. Ambrosia Health Food Store, everyone meets, off to parties. Row to Salt Lakes, raft skiffs together, smoke a joint, gaze at stars, float for hours. Lorrie Thompson's cabin, wet firewood, smoke in eyes, drip the clothes hang, rain beats on shingles.

Dory at Boat Bluff lighthouse, 1979.

French beret on Sebastian, quick draw artist, Erotic Poetry, outraged! Disqualified Carl's performance, licking Shiney's jell-o feet. Texas Bill's laughter, has us all captured.

Fed-Up Food Co-op, buckets of honey, bags of brown rice. James disappears, brings back Panama hats to Grenville Court hangout, Function

Junction parties. Dodge Cove path leads to Crippen Cove, Shelley and Bill's skiff ride to town in the morning.

1979. Move off the lights onto a boat, Rupert life at the docks, search for showers, odd jobs. Teach clay at the Civic, craft table sales, dinner sets and mugs. Mount Hays, ski hill restaurant, Dan dances the worm, private club, free fish, home to boat by dawn. Spiller brothers sit on topdeck, sailboat just launched, laughing 12-pack success. Rick builds *Rupert Pelican* at Cox's boatshed. Geoffrey on first *Pelican*, a rat in the bilge. Took it out for a rough sail, jumped off when docked, now he can sleep. Savoy, one too many after work, Hazel and I, madly bailing huge waves, *Margareta-of-the-Coffins*, hit shore at old sawmill site, long way from government dock. I ran down the boardwalk looking for help, fear is over, vibrating alive.

1980. Set course the Charlottes, land a job at Porcher,
Humpback Bay cannery. Caretakers Phil and Pat, new baby
Max, hand over the keys, left us
in history.

Dory with young friend Bronwyn at Humpback Bay Cannery, Porcher Island, 1981.

Tall narrow boatshed held up
with long pilings, pulleys on elevator ways, huge rusty cable un-
der lift tracks. Cannery dimness, dust motes floating in sun rays, cobwebs drape windows. Belt-driven drill press, metal lathe, tools. General store, walk-in wooden freezer, pop-up cash register. Bunkhouses, cookhouses, giant grills, oil stoves. Huge net lofts, badminton over the beam, fisher-men's net storage, deep hot tub in Japanese bunkhouse.

B.C. Packers tow over the Skeena gillnetter floats for the netmenders. American sailboats tie up at the dock, fresh glacier ice for drinks.

Fran and Steve, Feel Good Farm, wandering goats, chickens, homemade wine. Weaving studio, dolphins circle floor, boat covers, cushions, coats, spin wool, trade canned salmon for fleece. Dance class, ladies only. Law-yer lighthouse flashes into house at night, slow-mo disco. Lightkeepers Lance, Cathy, microphone recordings, whale songs passing. Peggy Carl's *Topolo*, two daughters, a goat, and a sinking floathouse.

Zoe, *Sailfish*, brewery on board, only woman on coast with abalone div-ing licence, Douglas in tow, piracy ruled. Her son Richard, *Clayoquot*, converted seiner, grandpa's sun house now a bunk, Oriental carpets, bathtub in hold, three pairs of parrots, one plays in his dreadlocks.

Carl, Sheila, *Tanleron*, junk sails yellow, red, blue, happiness glow, in setting sun. Thomas, Clara, tipping sail dory, the kids atop groceries, full to the gunnels, white rabbit, white mice, sail home, to Stephens.

Charley, Alice Ray, *Grandma*, lost and rescued, tossed and rescued, learning to sail. Paul saved *Secondhand Rose*, sunk in the winter, out from Salt Lakes hibernation, "which is the true reality? Night? Or day?"

One-Hook Dale is missing, his boat anchored quiet, in the bay he's found, wrapped in his anchor chain, very sad, private pain. Steve on the *Nid* sailed in, fresh mushroom picking, Queen Charlotte "silly" packed in honey, traded for tiller gear, homespun toque, clay mug. Laura, fairy-crew, layered in soft laughter.

Creek-walkers on their live-aboard boats, last of the fish counters, tell of bear scares, share dinners. Bob, Lee, one son per boat, youngest deckhands ever. "I'm not stupid, Olie, I'm Norwegian!" says Chris over C.B. radio. The whole fleet is entertained.

Old Japanese gillnetters, motoring from Port Edward, come for a hot tub bath, they built it long ago. Fingers in gills, hand a fresh salmon, scoop urchin eggs up with a spoon, offer salty taste. Their gifts offered with bows, thank you crinkled eyes smiling, the tubs heated and waiting.

Buildings blown apart, tin siding flapping, crashing gusts in the night, boatshed shakes bones, machine shop graveyard, trapdoor in floor, buried engines in mud, black pilings, shafts, flywheels rust. Last call for net storage, ripped-apart loft. Flotilla of old-timers into the dock, gathering of toolboxes, long-line, net twine, Japanese baskets, bowls. Gillnetters, red-nosed, teaching me to net mend, "open eye" mornings, scotch for the men, sherry for the lady. They know this life's at an end. Up the bay pinks stream by on the run, that's why it's called Humpback. A trail in the trees, Scottish shacks in salal, empty doorways, Mabel's ghost sells booze from her still, milk from her cow, scattered sheds now askew. Boat carcasses sunk into ribs, everything's of-use, fixable, you never know, rampant gardens fenced wide, plenty of goat cheese, fresh bread, tea by the fire. Splashes in dusk, pigs come swimming across tide, hungry for dinner, only snouts snorting ears, poke from saltwater. Lights shadow the dock, remittance man legend, Old Greyhill ties up Cherie. *Bent over black suit, gumboots, sou'wester hat. Heavy bottle-thick glasses, he can't see. Steps up the boardwalk, into stories long told, trailing tales, miss-beliefs. Thirty years of sail, from log-*

ging camps, lightstations, villages. To squatters, looters, boaters, and missing persons. Books lined the bulkhead, he penned the coast. For me his dire warnings: I'll be caught under the giant wood ball that grinds rock-worn holes. The draft dodgers dug tunnels carved too deep, I'll fall in and not climb out, no one will hear my calls for help. Those guys back then, built ships, hulls too long, beams to heavy, can't stay afloat, trapped in the boatshed, it'll lean over and crush you. "Don't go to Stephens," finger pointed at me. "You'll disappear forever and never be found."

1982. Stephens. Log cabin, cabana on stilts, sun bleached rock walk-ways, outdoor bathtub, fire underneath, stars overhead. Rowing skiff on clothesline, chickens follow shoreline, beans climb whale ribs, potatoes planted first, seaweed garden, water in bucket from stream across tide, wolves sing, roaring sea lions, surf on rocks, nights riotous. Row out the back door, watch the backflow of tide, jig a fish, bobbing dark log, turns one-eye towards me, silence deep, we look, lumpy nose, elephant seal. My skiff surges in swell, we both rise, we drop low, I lift oars to go.

Boatshed long, four-foot cedar shakes, adze chop marks, hand hewed, giant beams, forge in back, boats built narrow, all blown away, sunk into moss. Lenny sailed dory onto entrance rocks, three points rested on gun-nals, he crashed through trees, looking for help.

Wendy sailed *Mere-Nime* into town, just us two, newborn Bronwyn cry-ing in bunk. Xmas light candles on tree, Des and Wendy's cabin. Maggie, Elf, up the bay, babies growing, more on the way, for others, not me.

Started to build studio, searched for logs, endless survival, no time for my dreams. Joined the "real world."

On ferry 30 years soon to be over. Live in Masset old Catholic church. Commute to Rupert, fly across the Hecate. Tow Hill people, my younger reflection. Homes built of found things, into dunes, trees, stormy winters. Boat people, places I've lived, silence, hidden inlets. Rushing waterfalls, popping noise of low tide clams, rustling branches, birds calling, raven shouting, winds fill the silence. Shifting grey fog, ghostly boat shapes, navigation by sound. Names of grass knolls, untold battles, died lost, drowned, or dragged anchors. The stories disappeared in the mist, the trees, the dampness, moss covered past. Life up the coast, a drop in the ocean. Travel both worlds, the wind clears the head.

Gimli

by Betsy Cardell

GIMLI ACQUIRED ME AT the Sacramento Amimal Shelter in spring 1968. I have never encountered a more stolid and unflappable spirit. He promptly organized my life in ways I could not imagine.

Our first mission was to go to San Francisco. Gimli actually had his own agenda there. He would disappear and go off and do some Gimli thing somewhere. I encountered him once at Speedway Meadows in Golden Gate Park at a rock concert, far from where he had been left at home, across very busy lanes of traffic. He pretended he didn't know who I was.

Life became boring in San Franciso in 1970, so Gimli and I were off to Panama and Bolivia. When we returned, we loaded my grandmother's '56, two-tone, automatic transmission Chevy Bel Air in San Francisco and came to Canada in 1973.

Life was good.

We sold the Chevy, bought a very late vintage G.M.C. panel truck for $80, and signed up with a special N.D.P. program for over-qualified un-employable people to become teachers in rural places. We moved to the East Kootenays in 1974.

It was wonderful until it snowed and got very cold. Gimli did better in the Kootenay winter than I did. He had a fur coat. The panel truck did not have snow tires. I realized that we had made a terrible mistake. Applications to every school district on the coast were in the mail by early 1975. School District No. 50 made me an offer, and the Gimmer and I were headed for the the Queen Charlotte Islands.

We went to Mexico in the panel truck before we came to the Islands.

I remember vividly the trip over by float plane with Gimli on my lap from Prince Rupert to Masset to pick up the panel truck. It was a glorious trip across the Hecate Strait. The sun was shining and the water looked a warm tropical blue. On our way down-island we picked up a hitchhiker who was going to a place called Tlell. I asked directions to Queen Charlotte City.

Our first afternoon in Queen Charlotte City was a stunning late August day, crisp and clear. The School Board had a little grey house on the water that allowed dogs. We were met that first afternoon by two young ladies, Roberta and Tina, Grade 6 students, who helped unload the panel truck. It was full of house plants. The little house had wonderful windows and light. If I sat on my oil heater I could look out three sides and see the Inlet. The windows were soon covered with plants and we had arrived.

The Gimmer.

There was a trailer almost next door to the little grey house, full of fascinating women who had just come into town from the Burnaby Narrows. The arrival of an aging panel truck full of house plants had caught their notice and I was invited over. We were all getting on famously until they learned I was a teacher; the atmosphere cooled suddenly. Teachers, it seemed, were somewhat ostracized and did not tend to mingle with non-School Board types. When the new teachers first met the rest of the staff and the principal, we were told flat out we were not to go to the bar or to behave in an unseemly fashion. Gimli and I had certainly gotten around such restrictions in the past and proceeded to do the same in our new town.

We made wonderful friends. Nearby, Joline Martin was house-sitting for Karl and Carol Kulesha while they were fishing. After school, we would watch the *Northland Prince* go by with supplies. The boat would come so incredibly close to shore that it seemed practically in our laps. After the New Year, Jane Wilde arrived with her long skirts, down-to-earth/no-nonsense attitude and great sense of fun and adventure. Jane would make me lunch every day and in exchange would have baths at the little grey house. I think she was living in a plastic boat shed at the time.

Gimmer would travel along in the panel truck when I went to work and we would take walks during breaks. The panel truck met an unfortunate demise on the way to John and Jennifer's pottery studio up the highway, right after Christmas break. We hit a patch of black ice somewhere north of the village and I did all the wrong things, including not wearing a seat belt. We did a series of rolls on the side of the road, Gimli in the back with a loose pair of skis. When I looked back at one point in one of the rolls, it looked like Gimli and a couple of helicopter blades were revolving around in some amazing dance. We landed upright. Gimli was not pleased. We hitchhiked into town, dealt with the accident, and put on a very nice dinner party that evening.

Gimli had travelled internationally and did not recognize time zones or borders. He had made a life career as an escape artist. He would just disappear and it was always amazing where he would turn up, sometimes at an airport far from where he had last been seen. In 1978, I went off on a ski holiday to take a winter break from the Charlottes. Gimli did not make this trip and was left on Fleury Island with John and Buffy. When I came home and was dropped off at Margaret's Café by the airporter, Gimli was there to greet me, quite pleased with himself. I thought John must have been in town, so I went over to Bearskin Bay, the store he and Buffy owned, to touch base. I learned Gimli had disappeared from their place on Fleury Island that morning, walked around Lina Island and across Lina Narrows into town, to Margaret's, to meet me.

Gimli had no tolerance for guns. He got himself involved in a racoon hunt up toward Christie Bay. When shots were fired, Gimli disappeared. The hunters carried on up Skidegate Narrows, and when they returned, no Gimli. They now had to return to town to explain to me what had happened to the dog. When they got to the docks, Gimli was there to meet them. He had flagged down Art on the *Bilge Queen*, who came into shore and picked him up and brought him back to town. Art knew Gimli wasn't supposed to be out there by himself.

Gim loved the water. He thrived living on boats. He would go anywhere and everywhere, standing on the bow or walking the gunnels, just being out there. He did not mind being in the water, although it did almost cost him his life a couple of times. He made friends with all the cooks and was a welcome guest on the *Arrow Post*, a fisheries boat. He would plunge enthusiastically into creeks with spawning salmon and try to catch a few, or corral a salmon in a tide pool and play with it until the tide would come in. He loved the beach and would bark at the crabs as though he thought they could hear him.

Bears were not something that existed in Gimli's universe. —If a bear was beside him and he was beside you, he wouldn't tell you. He did this to George in Lagoon Inlet one fall. George had returned to where his skiff was beached. He was smoking a cigarette, sitting in the skiff with Gimli, both facing the stern. A bear was at the bow, right behind them, tearing apart a wastepaper basket.

In town, there was a bit of an arty thing happening. Bonnie and Marcia were putting together a production of *Alice in Wonderland* and had totally taken over Susie's house. There was talent coming up from Sewell Inlet: Lou Allison,

Betsy & Gimli in Haida Gwaii.

who played Alice. I was given the task of painting backdrops that would illustrate a "fall down the rabbit hole" experience. Gimli and I had just recently returned from the San Francisco Art Institute, (where Gim spent his 11th birthday locked up in a life drawing studio. He had been wandering San Francisco's North Beach and missed his ride home) and Bonnie and Marsha thought I could pull it off. I think I worked in Fran's boat shed. Gimli was the muse. The production was a huge success, the actors were stars, and all the shows sold out.

I feel so fortunate to have been a part of the wonderful and wild times in the seventies on the North Coast, particularly given my companion. Gimli went anywhere and everywhere and not always with me. Together, we shared many adventures and good times. We had many mutual friends, but also some of our own. On our journeys, we would often need a place to crash for either or both of us, somewhere safe where we could relax, be among friends, and get our act together. I know that not all the friends of my heart from the seventies were dog people, but they always welcomed Gimli.

From left: Betsy, Gimli & friends.

Still Hippying Around

by Margo Elfert

MY NAME WAS MARGO WATKINS when I came to the North Coast in my mid-twenties. I had spent the first 17 years of my life in Regina, Saskatchewan, but then my family moved to Brazil for a year when I was in Grade 12. I think that change did much to knock the prairie clods off my feet, and open my mind.

I went to University in Edmonton, where I studied biology. While there, I met a scientist who was doing research on the Queen Charlotte Islands, and found myself moving west, just for a summer at first, but then permanently.

One of the first memories I have is driving down the Skeena River between Terrace and Prince Rupert. The drive terrified me, with the narrow roadway between rail track and raging river. It was spring, and the river was high, alive with eagles. The valley was lush and the land didn't have the lines which made Alberta and Saskatchewan seem all "gridded up." It appeared free of such human restraints.

I had never really camped. My dad had grown up on the prairies without running water, and didn't consider it a holiday to "go without." But in the north I lived and thrived in a variety of camp-like abodes for many years. First, I lived in a Department of Fisheries cabin along the Tlell River, where my first visitors were Jehovah's Witnesses early on a Saturday morning. Next I lived at Mayer Lake in an old log cabin that was only accessible by boat. The move was expedited by liberating a small dock, pushing the tent trailer on board, and sailing it down the lake. In the morning while still anchored out in the lake, I heard an outboard, and a couple of fishermen: "George, I see a tent, and it's in the middle of the lake." I would have invited them for coffee, but the propane wasn't hooked up.

Later I lived in a cabin on Drizzle Lake. Both Mayer and Drizzle had totally habitable cabins, likely built around the turn of the century by settlers, who may have been disillusioned by the very muskeg that insured the survival of their cabins. They were so sound that I could stand inside while my partner expanded the windows with a huge chainsaw.

I was amazed at the abundance of places to inhabit free of charge, in a climate that was not nearly as extreme as the one in which I had spent most of my life.

I adapted pretty well to the new surroundings and environment, but I didn't like using large tools. My partner had a huge chainsaw that he used for all our needs. I couldn't lift it, let alone start it. I was lucky that we lived in the muskeg. There were numerous dead, spindly trees that had been killed by the acid bog. They were slow growing and dense, and I could easily kick them down and buck them up with my small Swede saw. They burned well.

After that relationship ended, I had to find a place to live for the winter of 1976. A friend let me take care of his 32-foot wooden halibut boat

Taking a break during herring season in Prince Rupert. Margo is second from the left.

that was tied up at the Masset dock. It was cozy – I could turn up the heat and put on the coffee without leaving my bunk. And I soon learned that if I tied it up one boat out from the dock, no inebriated visitors could stumble into my galley. Getting them out was impossible.

By the spring of 1977 I was broke, and borrowed enough money to go to Prince Rupert where I got a job at the Prince Rupert Fishermen's Co-op, pulling herring roe. During that spring I met many women who would become lifelong friends. I earned enough money to pay back my loan and go to Victoria to land another job for ecological reserves, this time on Rose Spit.

When I moved to Rose Spit with a young woman from Victoria on a research contract, I was able to use many of the skills I had gained. I could mend the leaking roof and repair the windows. I could install the cook stove and stove pipe. The beach was littered with both construction wood and firewood in all sizes. We could load up our backpacks and carry all the light, dry wood we needed to our cabin. We had a Swede saw and a small axe, tools that were my size. We were doing just fine, until the bosses from Victoria came.

It appeared to them that, although we had abundant firewood stored, we hadn't really done a serious wood trip. They insisted on dragging a couple of hernia-creating logs in from the beach, and the Swede saw and hatchet that had served us well for months were soon broken. I was told it was all because we didn't have the right tools. Well, we didn't any more.

We hiked to town every two weeks for supplies, mail, showers and beer. On more than one occasion as we headed out we saw a vehicle stranded on the beach, with no tire marks around it. It was usually a rental vehicle some unwitting tourists had been forced to abandon as the tide rose.

Few friends made the seven mile hike to the end of the Spit for a visit, so it was a surprise when the park warden drove out one day to announce that four people were hiking out to see us. They were naked. They turned out to be part of the Evelyn Roth Salmon Dance Troupe. We feasted on razor clams, our constant diet on the Spit, and then returned to Masset to take part, along with many Haida, in the dance. They said Rose Spit was almost as nice as Wreck Beach.

I loved the Charlottes, but had to move to Prince Rupert for work. I worked on a government grant at the museum for a couple of months in

November 1977. It was Iona Campagnolo time, and there were numerous grants to be had. I then got a job working at the Department of Fisheries in February 1978. I was the first female observer on domestic trawlers. My job included going to sea for one week a month, taking biological samples of groundfish.

I lived in a variety of abodes for my first year in Prince Ruper: a friend's attic, with no running water, and then another friend's house while he was out of town for a couple of months. I had an active social life, but I wasn't happy with life in town, and had many friends with boats who introduced me to Dodge Cove and Salt Lakes.

There was a little cabin at Salt Lakes that was vacant. It leaked, and had a lot of broken windows, but the community itself was very welcoming. Lorrie and Linda would be my neighbours. There was a skiff for sale, the *Cadillac*, but the owner was asking $1,500 for it. No one had paid more than $200 for a skiff and engine. I knew there was no way I could manage a full-time winter commute without it. This was one of the first big decisions I had ever made on my own, so I consulted the *I Ching*. With yarrow sticks I'd collected from Rose Spit, I threw my future. It told me: "It furthers one to cross the great waters. Pigs and fishes." I didn't understand the bit about pigs and fishes, but it was being as straight as it could with me about crossing the water. So I bought the *Cadillac*, truly a superior skiff, and a small Poulan chainsaw for my firewood, mended the roof and some windows again, and became an independent woman, with much community support, for 12 months. That was October 1978.

I was commuting to work every weekday. When I look back on it, it was

Margo's cabin at Salt Lake.

not the safest of situations. We had no communication with Prince Rupert, so no one would know if you left for work or decided to cancel due to bad weather. I moved there in October and had a long winter to learn skiffing skills. I knew the *Cadillac* could handle just about anything, but I had a personal limit. If the strap on my sou'wester was choking me by the time I got to Horse Head rock, halfway out the bay, I could come home until daylight.

The population at Salt Lakes was mixed. There were male and female singles and a few couples. I enjoyed going for coffee with the boys. Ken had the best coffee in the lakes: green beans he got from his travels in Central America roasted to perfection. I can still smell that toasty, fresh roasted aroma that would meet me as I approached on the beach.

We also had a senior in our community. He was called Blue Jesus, because he had a strong accent and when the blue jays would steal his food, he would come out on the porch and yell, "God damn dem blue jesus." We would take turns taking him to town for his shopping and mail runs, and he always bought us a case of beer. He came over for coffee one afternoon and showed us where he came from in Russia in a big atlas I had.

I enjoyed living on my own for that winter and the next summer. I had many close friends in the community, and we enjoyed sharing meals, exercise classes, crafting and gardening, and doing a lot of talking and coffee drinking together.

Early in 1979 I met Hans on a super trawler, the *Callistratus*, when I worked for the Department of Fisheries. We became friends when I was working on the boat. After my fisheries job ended I decided I was ready for a partner again. The *Callistratus* was anchored in the middle of Prince Rupert harbour, so I baked bread in my stovepipe oven, delivered it to Hans on the boat, and enticed him to supper. He arrived with a bottle of white wine in a bag of ice and a bottle of Cointreau. We ate abalone (legal then) that I'd just got at Stephens Island. He never left. I didn't realize until much later the bachelors were not happy with Hans' arrival – the stranger in the *Black Arrow* (an inflatable Bombardier skiff) who moved in on their territory. But they and everyone else there came to appreciate him in the community.

We both look back on the time we spent at Salt Lakes as very special. The community, the vista, the lifestyle was magical. By then we were in our early thirties, and we wanted to start a family. The one room cabin was too small, but we had scored some walls from a boatyard-teardown, and I hired our friend Gene to build an extension big enough for a bed on the back of the cabin. Hans was away in Vancouver with the *Callistratus* a lot at that time, but he came home for four days after the extension was complete, and Galen was conceived.

That summer I worked as an apprentice to Linda Gibbs, my neighbour, mending gillnets on the float that was anchored in our bay, behind Horse Head Rock. It was a very social place when the fleet came in. We would head out very early in the morning on Linda's boat, the *Naiad*. We had to wear scarves over our foreheads and cover up really well before the sun came up and after it went down, or we would be eaten alive by no-see-ums. We often got paid in fish that we couldn't always deal with because we were too busy mending nets. There was no refrigeration. Our friend Stu canned some of it for a cut of the fish.

Galen (meaning "calm sea") was born the following February. He is, astrologically, a Pisces Pig, so the *I Ching* was totally right. He was the first baby to be born at the Lakes in our close circle of friends. In his first week of life, a wonderful, beautiful troop of women came up the beach, laughing and proud to bring the quilt they had made for him, along with a bottle of wine. Galen still has the quilt.

We were very comfortable at Salt Lake. Hans hooked up a generator to run the washer spin dryer. We had propane and electric lights, a wonderful sound system, a convection oven and a Paloma water heater. Life was good, but the space wasn't big enough for two children and we wanted a second baby. When a position caretaking a house and the C.B.C. transmitting station high on a hill became available, we moved there.

The move was eventful. C.B.C. was transporting some materials to the site via helicopter, so we crated up all our belongings, put them on a barge, and towed them to the base of the hill. It was August, and we were hit by one of the electrical storms common at that time of year, hit us. Kristin Miller, who lived across the bay at Salt Lake, was on the barge for the ride. It had been pouring rain, but Kristin's soaking wet hair started to stand straight out from her head. I was sure she was in line for a major bolt of lightening. We got her to put her head into one of the tire bumpers on the barge, and her hair went down again.

Now we were on the electrical grid and had two bedrooms, so we felt totally spoiled. We purchased a small A.T.V. to make the trek to and from the dock easier, and had another baby — Dylan (meaning "the sea"). We stayed there six years, when once again work made us move. We've been in or around Vancouver ever since.

Soon after we arrived south, I started to meet with northern friends who had migrated to Vancouver. Despite our busy lives, the Yin and Yang Yoga Group, yoga followed by a beer at the Wise Hall with many of the women I met in Prince Rupert in 1977, has been meeting for over 20 years. It's an important weekly check-in that keeps us in close touch.

The first four summers after our move, we returned to Dodge Cove for the month of August. It was a place where the boys could learn responsibility. In the city they had to be held too close; there was no room for independent decision making. In Dodge they had a large extended family that knew and loved them, as well as their own rowboat and bikes, and could get into a little mischief without the same level of risk as in Vancouver.

I haven't been back north for a visit in a while. I do end up on Haida Gwaii most years during the Sablefish Tagging Charter, where I have been the chief biologist since 2000. Yes, I did get back to sea. And Hans and I look forward to spending time up there once we're retired. We now live on a 40-foot, tri-cabin cruiser — the *Roamin'* — that we bought in 2008 and rebuilt, currently moored in Richmond. We've been living aboard her since October 2010, and are enjoying it thoroughly. The time I spent on the north coast in my twenties has left me more open to the unorthodox.

Boating in Paradise

by Barb Rowsell

IN THE EARLY 1970S, my husband Keith and I were living on the west coast of Vancouver Island, in the Nitinat area. Nitinat, like Haida Gwaii, is a very special and beautiful place: home to aboriginal people for centuries. Europeans came there at the turn of the twentieth century. It was promoted by a steamship line as a Mediterranean-style resort area and lots were sold worldwide. It certainly has the beaches and beauty, but, unfortunately for those who came, not the clientele or the climate. One poor gentleman from France literally starved to death as there was no one to buy his flowers that he grew or understand his French. Our dear friend Ed came with his family as a small boy and stayed on. He was a logger who worked in the heyday of logging in the Discovery Passage area and returned to Nitinat to work in a small logging camp on the lake. He was a lifelong student of the natural world and of people. He took us greenhorns under his wing and became our mentor on the history and natural world of Nitinat.

Our other neighbours (we were all separated by several miles by water and/or footpaths) were a native family who were sometimes at Whyac, the village at the Nitinat mouth. A few months before our son Joshua was born, they lost two sons, young men, when their dugout rolled over travelling down Nitinat Lake at night. Their mother said Josh was the reincarnation of her sons and would often come to visit him. Anyone who knows Josh will agree that it is quite possible that he has two energetic young men in him.

By 1975, we were bushed and looking for a bit more civilization, when an opportunity came up. Bill Reid wanted to donate a pole and longhouse to Skidegate and was working with a mutual friend, named Rudy, on the project. We had worked for Rudy at Nitinat cutting seven tons of large cedar panels that were the backdrops for the northwest native display in the new Museum of Man in Gatineau. We had cut the wood with a large Alaska bushmill and he wanted the longhouse wood cut with that. How can you turn down an offer like that? It seemed like a good idea at the time, a one-year contract. We decided to make the move.

At Nitinat we travelled by water, 14 miles down Nitinat Lake from the logging roads that went to Lake Cowichan or Port Alberni. We loved being on the water and were looking forward to getting a larger boat. At Nitinat we had been limited to one that we could land and pull up the beach out of the surf and get over the infamous Nitinat Bar. We were excited about the boating possibilities on the Charlottes.

It was very nice to live in a community of people and be earning money, something always in short supply at Nitinat. Our plan was to make some money, get a boat and find another remote place here on the Charlottes. Having kids in school, earning a living, and life in general kept that at bay. We were part of the group that bought the old whaling station at Rose Harbour. That looked like the dream place but we soon realized that the cost and effort of maintaining it ourselves would be very high.

Life was very exciting on the Queen Charlottes, there was so much on the go in the seventies, especially for bushed people used to being alone. People were rebuilding old boats, building new boats, building house barges, living in remote places, learning to fish, or just heading off to explore these amazing islands. No one had much money but there were always lots of willing hands to help with projects, and innovative making-do was never in short supply.

Barb and Keith in the Charlottes.

We had bought a 38-foot halibut boat to get back and forth to Rose Harbour, about 100 miles south from the Village of Queen Charlotte. We were commercially fishing and chartering and realized that the boat was fairly comfortable, had most of the mod cons, and was a less expensive lifestyle than living in a remote shoreside. On a boat you own whichever inlet you are in and if you don't like the neighbours, up anchor and away. And so in 1984 we began the construction of a new floating home, the *Anvil Cove*, a 53-foot steel schooner.

We launched *Anvil Cove* in 1990 and it has earned our living ever

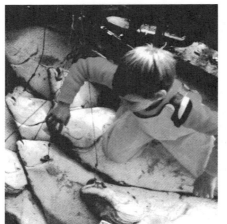

Josh helps with a halibut catch.

since. We had built a larger boat thinking that we could put everything on it and not need to own property as well. When we had both property and boat, whatever you needed was at the other place and whichever we were working on, the other was neglected. Murphy's Law, things take on a life of their own; a bigger boat just means more stuff to keep it happy.

We started doing Department of Fisheries contract charters and quickly started to add other research work. With a boat *Anvil Cove's* size, we could comfortably take groups of people, and with our experience of the Islands we were quite busy. We have taken researchers to Gwaii Haanas National Park, mappers for the terrestrial area, archeologists, intertidal mappers, seabird biologists, underwater geologists as well as R.C.M.P. members, Telus, workers with the Department of Fisheries & Oceans, and commercial divers. The researchers are the best, you get to ask them all your dumb questions. We always learn a lot.

One of my favourite stories from those days was a trip with researchers doing the terrestrial baseline for Gwaii Haanas. We were on the west coast of Moresby Island and one of the guys had forgotten his backpack in the last inlet. Keith suggested jumping in the skiff to go back: it was faster than running in the big boat and the rest of us would continue on to the next inlet. There had been a storm and there was still a big swell running, which wasn't really apparent until they went to get in the skiff; it was above the deck and then 10 feet down. But they got in and went off. We continued on to Mike Inlet. This part of Moresby is steep, rocky, mountains dropping straight into the sea and with the big seas crashing off solid rock it is a bit daunting. Mike Inlet has a funny opening: it looks as though you are running straight into this rock wall and then it opens and you are in. It wasn't until many months later that I realized that the wheelhouse had become very quiet and the sidelong glances from the remaining guys was a measure of their apprehension of the situation. Remote west coast, big seas, running into a rock wall, all with a woman in charge. To their credit no one said a thing. I still laugh at this memory.

When Gwaii Haanas was created, visitors started to come. We first started working in tourism transporting independent kayakers to Gwaii Haanas. Sometimes when it came time to unload at their destination on a rainy evening it was hard to pry their tiny fingers from the warm, dry boat. "Can't you just stay with us and we'll paddle during the day and come back to the boat in the evening?" was a common question. And so the concept of kayak mothership was born. That was 20 years ago and here we are still.

Is there still any remnant of the dream that brought us here? I'd say so. We are hoping to sell the business so we can buy another boat (no time left to build) and keep exploring the coast without guests, or at least guests that will move at our pace. The guests are wonderful; we have met some lovely people, but sometimes you just want to spend a whole week in one inlet, not always going to the "necessary" places. We would like to spend more time on the rest of the B.C. coast too. Way too much coastline left to visit.

My recreation has always been to paddle and hike as often as I can with my friends in easily accessible places. That is certainly one of the great things about Haida Gwaii: it is so easy to get to fabulous, wild places for day trips. And such wonderful people who are willing to share that with me.

A float

by Lou Allison

I DIDN'T SET OUT TO join a movement or become part of a trend: I simply cut myself loose from the moorings of my life. I grew up in Ottawa, half French-Canadian, half Scot-Irish descent, a common blend in eastern Ontario, farmer stock on both sides but now middle-class, with an accountant father and a stay-at-home mother. My birth mother died of cancer when I was 8 (the poor woman was only 38 with three children, 8, 6 and 3, and my heart aches for her). My father remarried, to a woman who had two teenage children, and surprisingly, they had another. My large blended family was unusual for that time and place. Exotically, we were even of two religions, though my Anglican step-siblings were expected to attend Catholic mass along with the rest of us. I often felt alone and misunderstood, mandatory feelings for adolescents, but isolating and painful nonetheless. No one shared my tastes and interests in poetry, singer-songwriters, coffeehouses, and literary novels, as I mooched around in black clothes, long scarves and shawls tied over my coats. I had an after-school job filing in a sales office, answering the phone and dealing with the inflated egos of the on-the-road salesmen. Hardly the stuff of romance, I felt. I harboured restlessness, whetted by the sight and sound of the trains that wailed as they came and went from the new station that went up in the empty fields near my workplace. Because I had academic prize money and am inherently thrifty, I attended one year in an arts program at the University of Ottawa, falling asleep from boredom in the large lecture halls, looking out the windows, and skating home along the Rideau Canal, dreaming of the river I could "skate away on." So, I saved my money and by midsummer 1973, at the age of 18, I quit my job, bought a train ticket to Vancouver and left for good.

I stopped to visit a school friend and her grandmother at a cottage on the Georgian Bay, and, while there, my friend Val called to tell me that she couldn't stand it, she wanted to come too, to wait for her there, she was catching a bus. So, two young girls stood at the whistle stop at French Creek sat upright in coach seats with terrible sunburns caught while sleeping off hangovers in the sun after a wild night of drinking, rolled their Drum tobacco cigarettes and watched the unending scroll of scenery of a cross-Canada train trip. Cue the soundtrack. With every lovely mile, I was getting further from the life I had been groomed for by the expectations of my parents and my own academic success.

Cut loose, I rattled around British Columbia, camping mostly and meeting people. Eventually I fell in love with a man named Tiwill when he played hours of classical music for me on a piano in a shed with slatted walls that let in long slanting beams of dusty sunlight. We went back to Quebec for the winter, but eventually longed for B.C. We left again on a train from the Ottawa station. My father cried when he took us to the station: I have thought of that often over the years.

Eventually we ended up on the beach in Lund, and I fell in love with the ocean, hard, fast and permanently. I have lived at its edge ever since. We picked fruit in the Okanagan to earn the money to buy a canoe, and then made a five-week paddling trip to the Brem River at the end of Toba Inlet, circling islands, battling fierce tides and camping on tiny beaches within inches of high tide. The second summer in the orchard, I conceived a child. We married and thought more seriously about work. Rumours of the magical and mystical Queen Charlotte Islands tickled our imaginations, so Tiwill got a job as a chokerman in a logging camp there. I was to follow once he was settled.

My first thought on landing in Sandspit was: "where are the arbutus trees?" I was that ignorant that the north coast is not like the south, notatall notatall girlie. And living in Sewell Inlet in a remote logging camp was not like swimming naked in a lake on Cortes Island or living in a borrowed tipi in Okeover Inlet. The culture shock could not have been more profound if I had landed in Pago Pago, both to the middle class

Ottawa girl and the itinerant hippie chick. While the child grew within me, I walked miles along steep, wet gravel roads, diving for the side whenever the huge overloaded logging trucks thundered by. The woods were huge, dark, damp and dripping, wherever they weren't logged to a clearcut devastation. The other wives in the married quarters were kind to the little thing in beads, headband and overalls, but I was profoundly lonely, lonelier than I have ever been before or since. And my thoughts turned more and more to where to have the baby.

✳   ✳   ✳   ✳

At that time, this world of behemoth log trucks, towering dripping forests interspersed with the devastation of cut blocks and long solitary days broken by the highlights of the monthly arrival of the *Northland Prince* with supplies, the visiting public health nurse who flew in for clinics and twice-weekly mail made up the entirety of my experience of the mystical Queen Charlotte Islands. Gradually however, another world was slowly revealing itself. Itinerant boats tied to the small stiff-leg dock sometimes for days at a time: a lot of people on small boats were washing around the Islands in those adventurous days. I eventually got to know some of them. I heard of a woman named Agate, who was interested in becoming a midwife, and who lived in a houseboat at the dock at Moresby Camp, north of Sewell, at the end of a dirt road. We visited her, her partner "old man," and their two big yellow dogs. I loved her warmth and strength, her wide smile, laughter-lit eyes, and strong tanned hands. In Queen Charlotte City, I met a woman named Gail who offered her small octagonal log house at the top of Hippie Hill for the birth. Gail's neighbour Stas was learning acupuncture. My friend Patrick Star was squatting on the beach in a funky home-built camper that had an extra bunk: I could stay with him while I waited. A few weeks before the due date, I came out of camp, stayed with Patrick and walked and walked, up and down the road, picking salmonberries and inky-cap mushrooms and wild greens, whiling away time in the tiny lovely cemetery at the end of the road, meeting people, and waiting. The baby arrived about two weeks late, but on July 10, 1976, Simon was born in that little cabin perched among the treetops: Agate caught him, the first of the many babies she would eventually deliver, and Stas did acupressure (I remember the pressure of his strong hands on my feet): the first baby for all of us. I was 21 years old. Four days later my little family flew back to camp.

We moved out of Sewell when Simon was five months old. Del, who owned a barge, was towing it by and kindly loaded our motley, meager possessions aboard and we made the long sea-journey out around Cumshewa Head and north to Queen Charlotte City. We set up to build a trimaran: there was a fashion in them at the time. When our marriage foundered a couple of years later, Tiwill ended up with the boat. A few months later, when Simon was 2 $\frac{1}{2}$, he and I moved aboard the *Azurite*, a 65-foot ex-survey boat for a mining company, ex-halibut boat, ex-fish-packer built in 1912, owned by Jeremiah, a big handsome man with a long ponytail that reached halfway down his broad back. We left the dock in Queen Charlotte City on December 3, 1978, for a two week voyage to what is now the Gwaii Haanas National Park. We came back seven weeks later, out of everything except brown rice and onions.

Lou with son Simon in Queen Charlotte City in 1977.

Thirty-four years later, I am still here. Jeremiah and I lived in what is now officially called Haida Gwaii for two more years, on venison, fish and clams, and a bare subsistence income from occasional and seasonal jobs. We brought the old *Azurite* across Hecate Strait to go work in the Khutzeymateen (also now a park) at helicopter logging: he fell trees and I bull-cooked, cleaning bunkhouses. We moved to Oona River on Porcher Island and began the long process of building our present boat, the *Far Reach*. We had a baby, a girl this time, named Jeannine for my young mother who had died so many years earlier. We bought a tiny old floathouse, expanded, crudely refurbished and moved it onto a new raft. For the next several years, we towed it up and down the coast, handlogging, pulling logs into the water with a boat, at Wales Island, inside the Alaska panhandle on the Canadian side, at the bottom of Grenville Channel at Union Pass and places in between. Sometimes, the claim was ours; sometimes we worked for other small-time operators. We worked for one of the last A-frames operating on the coast: an A-frame is just that, a

tall capital-A structure on a log raft, set up with a donkey engine and the rigging to pull logs from cut-blocks along the water's edge. Jeremiah fell and I did dishes and taught correspondence school to the owners' children, along with Simon who was in Grade 1. We tied our floating house alongside the barges that housed the bunk-house, cookhouse, generator-shed and owners' trailer. We worked shows in Cornwall Inlet, and later in Klewnuggit and Kxngeal Inlets along Grenville Channel. We

Lou (at left) aboard the "Cape Bell ferry" in 1977.

sometimes got jobs because of our mobility: we would be the first on site, Jeremiah falling ahead of the crew, me at anchor with the kids, listening dry-mouthed for the sound of his saw. When it was quiet as he filed the chain and gassed up, I would torture myself with imaginings of his broken body under a limb or tree. We lived for quite a while in Kumealon Inlet, again in Grenville: we moored the house across from the camp and Jeremiah took a skiff to work. I used to row across with the kids and two weeks of laundry every time the camp shut down: that camp was called a "10-and-4," ten days operating, four days shut down when all the crews would fly out, leaving behind the watchman, his dog, and us. And from time to time, between jobs, we returned to Oona River, tying to one or other dock there; we centred around that tiny isolated village for eight years.

Eventually, we moved our floathouse to Humpback Bay and beached it up the estuary, where it remained for 17 years. Now we just took the *Far Reach* when we left for work, coming and going like swallows to a nest box. Those years were very happy, with a stable home base: the friends who had invited us there because they wanted neighbours became our family. I grew a huge subsistence garden, and with salmon to can and smoke, clams and shrimp and octopus, the animals our neighbours raised, and the deer Jeremiah hunted, as well as yearly food orders, we always had a full pantry. We spent part of each year on the boat on various jobs, ranging far, covering the coast from north of Vancouver Island to within sight of Alaska, and, my favourite, returning often to the Beloved Islands, Haida Gwaii. We were alone a lot, but we also had friends stretched in a long interconnected web up and down the coast, the long wild coast with names as beautiful as its bays, coves, inlets, islands and passages.

Simon left to live with his father in Maine when he was 15. Jeremiah's sister Eunice and her daughter Alicia moved up from Washington State and Eunice married our neighbour. Eventually, both girls also decided to leave for school: Alicia went to the eastern U.S. to relatives there, and Jeannine and I moved to Prince Rupert, then Victoria until she graduated from high school. When she too had flown the coop, and I returned to the floathouse, the silence echoed and the air lay heavy and lifeless without the kids racketing around. Life is nothing if not change, the saying goes, and our life in Humpback Bay, which we had thought so stable and permanent, changed too.

On a still October morning in 2005, Jeremiah and I towed the floathouse, a raft with our outbuildings, a barge with Jeremiah's antique John Deere crawler, and a herring punt with lumber, ladders and a heap of oddments with a few logs and a skiff in a long motley train, across Cha-

Lou & Jeremiah towing across Chatham Sound to Dodge Cove in 2005.

tham Sound to Dodge Cove on Digby Island across from Prince Rupert, like a floating *Beverly Hillbillies* re-make. We had bought a piece of land with a shacky house and some rough acreage next to it, so we beached the works there, and settled in to become townies after our decades out. Though not everyone thinks of Dodge Cove as "town," we do: we live in sight and sound of other houses; we have electricity, running water, a phone and Internet; and we no longer look out an inky black sky at night.

I now work at the Prince Rupert Library, the first job I ever got on my own since taking up with Jeremiah at the age of 24. It is a whole new life, with a new set of demands, challenges and rewards. I bring the sum of my experience to my present life: the B.A. in English I got by correspondence, studying for years at night by kerosene lamp, a picture from a bygone century; the habit of self-directed work; and a lifelong love of reading. I am happy to be in contact with so many diverse and interesting people after so many solitary years. I am a committed north coaster. I deeply love where I live, and, though I sometimes regret no longer being beyond the fringe, soaking the land, sky and seascapes into my psyche, I have large windows that give onto the harbour, I still have a big vegetable garden and I get to take my little boat across the harbour to town. Sometimes I throttle back to make the trip take longer. I look at the sky with its scudding clouds and the play of light on the water, and I know that I am still on the same ocean that wraps around all the islands near and far and me too.

My American Girlfriends

by Jane Wilde

THERE I WAS, A TEENAGER in southern Ontario, reading and hearing about Woodstock, Fleetwood Mac and people moving back to the land, eager to leave my comfortable and happy home and restless to get going with my life. Only now I'm learning that there was a whole continent of restless young women out there the same as me.

I wanted adventure. As soon as possible after I finished some college I joined the youth exodus to B.C. from southern Ontario. B.C. was a magnet drawing young travellers west, and I joined in along with my childhood friend Lenny. I attended university in Victoria. Lenny kept travelling and later invited me to join him in Queen Charlotte City (or, as we called it, Charlotte) where he was building a sailboat. He had sailed to Charlotte from Hawaii and his stories of his life and community there were so compelling that I wanted to visit. I was eager to take him up on his offer of a place to stay.

Knowing I was planning to go north, my Mom, who was concerned about my ongoing unemployment, urged me to apply for a high school teaching job in Charlotte that she had noticed advertised in the Vancouver newspaper. Though not a teacher, I was successful in my application due to the serious teacher shortage at the time, especially in this remote northern community. In January 1976, I was hired to teach home economics for the rest of that term. I was 21 and sensed that my adventure was finally beginning. I had no idea what big changes were ahead for me.

Arriving in Charlotte to start my new job, I spent my first night at the dock sleeping on a sailboat, filled with excitement at the strangely different place I found myself. The rocking of the waves, the sounds of the creaking boat rigging, and the smell of the ocean all combined to keep me awake with excited anticipation about my new life ahead. Lenny very quickly helped me get settled and smoothed my way into a very welcoming and diverse community of other new arrivals from all over North America whom he had befriended since his arrival.

Though I knew I was going to an island off the north coast of B.C. and had found it on a map, I had no idea how isolated it was, what the community was like, or how rich and intense my life there would become. And the isolation became a valued feature for me, further insulating the uniqueness of our community.

There was not yet a B.C. Ferries service, so getting on and off the islands was complicated. The options were: an expensive Air Canada flight via Vancouver; the weekly *Northland Prince* passenger and freight boat; or driving to Masset, barging the car to Prince Rupert, taking a float plane yourself across Hecate Strait and spending a night or two at the colourful Inlander Hotel, hoping the sheets had been changed recently, waiting for the car to arrive before hitting the road.

Charlotte did not have a lot of services, but the basics were covered. The *Northland Prince* at the dock signalled to the community the arrival of fresh food in the grocery store. The dairy and produce disappeared quickly, so we needed to plan shopping accordingly. There were other delicious options though, like fresh seafood. Feasts of abalone were still possible then because they had not yet been over-harvested. I had a simple wardrobe and found that gumboots worked well with dresses but not for dancing. Charlisle's, the local store, carried the essential wool clothes and raingear in a limited variety of styles and colors. We all wore the same sorts of rustic outfits and with our own sense of coastal rainforest fashion.

In my first days of working as a teacher, I was quickly identified as a rookie by my co-workers and students due to my lack of credentials and experience, as well as being a new face in a small town. I'm sure my ignorance about the full scope of what I had agreed to take on in my new teaching job saved me. I was naïve and eager at the same time. Some days I questioned my choice to take the job, as my teenaged students, some only a few years younger than me, hung over the fridge door in the home economics classroom, wondering aloud what there was to eat, having just let themselves in through the locked door with a plastic comb. My survival goal for the term was to just keep everyone busy cooking, eating and sewing. I did completely leave out the required theory part of the curriculum, much to the dismay of the real home economics teacher who inherited my unruly, hungry students for the next term.

Fortunately for me, by the end of my first week of teaching I was adopted by my co-workers Betsy and Joline. They were real, qualified teachers, they were confident, and they could see I needed help. And help me they did, with lesson plans, parties, men, music and life. They shared with me their perspectives of being well-educated American women who had already travelled the world, with careers as well as exciting life experiences that I had not. Betsy had lived at Haight-Ashbury, Joline grew up near Chicago, and they too ended up in Charlotte looking for adventure. They opened my eyes to the big world through their friendship.

I was intensely happy, with a sense of freedom and independence, and strong friendships. My new community offered me a wide variety of adventures. I was lucky to accompany a school field trip by float plane to three southern historic Haida villages with some totem poles still standing. I travelled to remote beaches in boats, swam in the ocean, lived in a float house, and, for a short time, in a tiny plastic-covered cabin next to Lenny's big boatshed.

At the same time the sexual revolution was raging around us in Charlotte.

My own hormones, along with those of the larger migrant community, ensured lively dances at Skidegate Hall, beach parties, romances, split-ups, reconciliations, and relocations, all with not-to-be-missed drama. I heard the terms "the Charlotte shuffle" and the "spring and fall shuffle" for the first time here, referring to the pat-

Jane & Lenny in the boathouse, 1977.

tern of relationships ending and reforming with new combinations of partners over the course of the year. Mostly it was exciting, free-spirited and mutual, but there were a number of broken hearts and confused children over the years as we struggled to sort out the balance of freedom and commitment.

I became interested in learning more about birth control and sexuality during this time and I memorized the then popular books *The McGill Birth Control Handbook* and *Our Bodies, Ourselves*. Birth control methods were still mostly unreliable or unpleasant and were a constant topic of conversation and angst among the women. We supported each other through I.U.D. insertions (intrauterine device) and late periods. Pregnancies both wanted and unwanted were ongoing sources of joy and pain.

My third American friend Agate, who came from California, helped set the course for my career and much of my life's work in reproductive health. She seemed so exotic and striking, and she was so warm and friendly. She would return to her home in Tlell from her visits south with all kinds of new things like artichokes, Fry boots, and a copy of the recently published *Spiritual Midwifery*. Agate was a midwife who helped women with home births. One day she asked me if I would be interested in being her helper at an upcoming birth since her usual helper was unavailable. I had no idea what to expect, or even really what to do except act helpful. When I saw that little baby's head appear, as the mother seemed to be happily expecting and as Agate seemed to be calmly anticipating, I was amazed. Seeing that first birth profoundly affected me. From that moment, I found my direction, passion and career focus. I attended two more home births with Agate and started to think that maybe being a maternity nurse would allow me to work with women having babies and learn more about all aspects of reproduction.

Jane at her first birth with Agate, 1978.

By then I had changed jobs several times and was working as a server at the Queen Charlotte Hotel bar. It was fun, especially during fishing season when the tips were generous — bags of $100 bills were legendary during herring season — but I couldn't see myself making a career of it. I applied to nursing school and was eventually accepted despite my advanced age (24) and my poor math and science marks. At that time, nursing schools were more welcoming to mature students with some life experience, and I had both by then, including a strong interest in focusing my studies on reproductive health.

I left Charlotte in the summer of 1979 from the same dock that I had arrived at three years earlier. I was still restless, on my way to more adventures at nursing school, transformed by my intense life experiences on the Islands.

I finished nursing school, became a maternity nurse, and returned to the north coast to work in Prince Rupert. I met my partner Richard in my new town. He too had come west from Ontario in the same 1970s migration, along with many of our long-time friends. We have two grown-up daughters who have taught me the full meaning of reproduction from the joys of conception, through the intensity of parenthood, to the mixed emotions of our empty nest.

Today I am still on the North Coast, on the other, eastern side of Hecate Strait from my original landing in Charlotte 36 years ago. My time is divided between homes in Dodge Cove and Prince Rupert, alternately cursing the rain and appreciating the rich life and long-time connections I have here. I have adventures in different ways now with family transitions, my nursing career, and fabric art explorations.

At my core, I'm still restless. My three American girlfriends have been there for me through it all, as they still are today.

Jane (second from right) says good-bye to Queen Charlotte City in 1979, from the same dock she arrived at three years earlier. Also pictured are (from left) Nancy and American girlfriends Joline & Betsy.

All the Wrong Reasons

by Carmen Ross

THE YEAR WAS 1976 WHEN I went north for one bad reason: sex.

Well maybe not just sex. I had gone to the Queen Charlotte Islands the year before to visit my good friend Linda who was teaching there. I had a great visit with her and met some new friends like Jane, Big Bill and Lenny, and I thought it was quite the place, full of young people all talking about freedom and dreams. Pretty heady stuff really. People were looking for freedom from the binding restrictions of the lives of their parents, freedom from social mores, gender inequity, the 9-to-5 work week, parental expectations, dirty wars and dirty tricks; dreams of new lives, new values, community, co-operation, the Age of Aquarius in the rain soaked forests of western Canada. It all seemed a possibility in this far-flung place.

But there was the sex, too. I had been a goody two-shoes all my life, going to school, working part-time at hope grinding jobs, always doing as I was asked. I was following in my mother's shoes, training to be a nurse and trying to find the perfect boy to meet her expectations when everything seemed to fall apart. My perfect boy, destined for glory and law school, was playing me along while shopping for his Miss Perfect. When I found out I was devastated and demoralized. Had I been wearing blinkers? Had my whole life been constrained by a long dark tunnel without vision? I desperately needed to change my ways and break out of the mold. So I thought: why not head back to where dreams seemed possible, and while I was trying to find out what my own particular dream might be, have a little sex, well maybe a lot of sex, with someone the complete opposite of my perfectly flawed boy. That was it! I was looking for a bad boy, and if the Queen Charlottes had anything, they had one heck of a lot of bad boys!

I arrived in Queen Charlotte City full of great expectations and bad wardrobe selections. How long do an alpaca poncho and red leather boots last in the Misty Isles? For that matter, how long does red hair dye last? Right away I was met by good and friendly people.

"Need a place to stay? No problem, stay at my house while I go visit Agate Annie."

"Great – who?"

"Need a place to work? No problem, try the hospital, Dr. T is always looking for new girls."

"Great – what?"

Welcoming faces were everywhere, and I was soon whisked into the strangest social whirlwind. How about a date poling across the Tlell River to share intoxicating conversation and fumes with politically astute people? Or how about scrambling along a cobblestone beach for over a mile, in the dark, to find a cabin floating precariously on a raft of logs, navigate over the gangway by feel, and be welcomed in without hesitation for tea by candlelight? The poncho, boots, and red hair dye soon dissolved but the warm welcome didn't. In fact there were so many friendly faces I was about to give up ever finding that bad boy.

But one should never give up too easily. That midnight stroll on the beach had led me to a little floating cabin of a very promising possibility. He was tall, had long dark hair, a bushy beard, and piercing eyes, rough on the edges and not too smooth on the inside either. Could this be the bad boy? He did look a lot like Charles Manson, but then so did half the guys on this rock! At least he certainly didn't fit into any city mold I had encountered. He had a deer hung in the trees, fish frying on the stove and was building a boat. Again, so were half the guys I had met so far, but then something happened that stirred my heart. He introduced me to two beautiful little girls, his neighbours and his friends. He told me that he had met them in Hawaii when he had crewed on their parents' sailboat. They had sailed from that tropical paradise together and had been close ever since. A guy like this may not be the bad boy I was looking for, but my curiosity overcame my preconceived predilections.

I'm glad my curiosity won the day because what a romantic life we created for each other. I will never forget skinny-dipping in the cold moonlit seas right off our front porch. Warming up together in the single cot, really only room for one, but I mentioned the sex goal right? Hikes to the coast, the long beaches below Tow Hill, the quiet forest glades with that deep magical moss as soft as feather pillow perfect for... any goal you could dream of. Fantastic feasts of scrumptious seafood gathered by friends and shared around a roaring fire. We were not rich but we lived a rich life and could ask for very little more.

Time sped by and not long later we got married on the beach, wind in our hair and all those friendly people at our side. What characters they were. A German octogenarian, who claimed she was family even though we were worlds and ages apart, carefully helped with the groom's wardrobe. Our landlord, a trapper right out of the tales of the *coureurs de bois*, who fed us seagull eggs, beaver tail and beans, and bear pot roast and gave us a wedding gift of, what else, a beaver skin pelt. In the blink of the eye we had a little boy (I did mention the sex, right?). Our dreams had grown and changed together, to having a family, boat, friends, travel and work.

Before long we sailed away on our new home, sad to leave so much behind but happy to start on the next leg of our life journey together. To-

The wedding day on the shore of Skidegate Inlet.

day our boy has become a man. Grandchildren play at our feet. Those little girls I met on the beach are beautiful women who still share their lives with us. We travel to far-flung destinations and work hard to achieve our goals: helping children, caring for the world, and

The bad boy, the good girl, and the baby, Christmas 1978.

working for positive change. Much has been accomplished and much is left to do, but we are forever thankful for that wonderous place, hidden in the storm-tossed seas and shielded by the grey fog that somehow helped us change our lives and create a dream that we are still living today. Not bad after all, for the girl who headed north for all the wrong reasons.

Prince Rupert

and environs

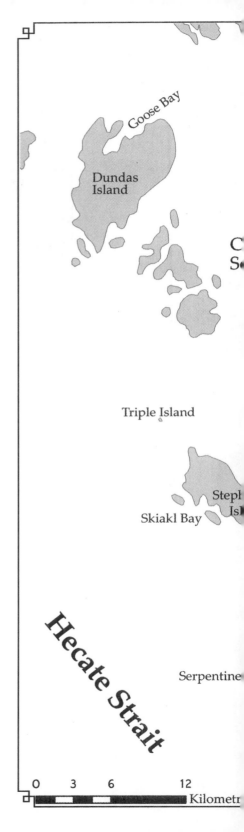

Goose Bay

Dundas
Island

C
S

Triple Island

Steph
Is

Skiakl Bay

Serpentine

Hecate Strait

0   3   6   12
Kilometr

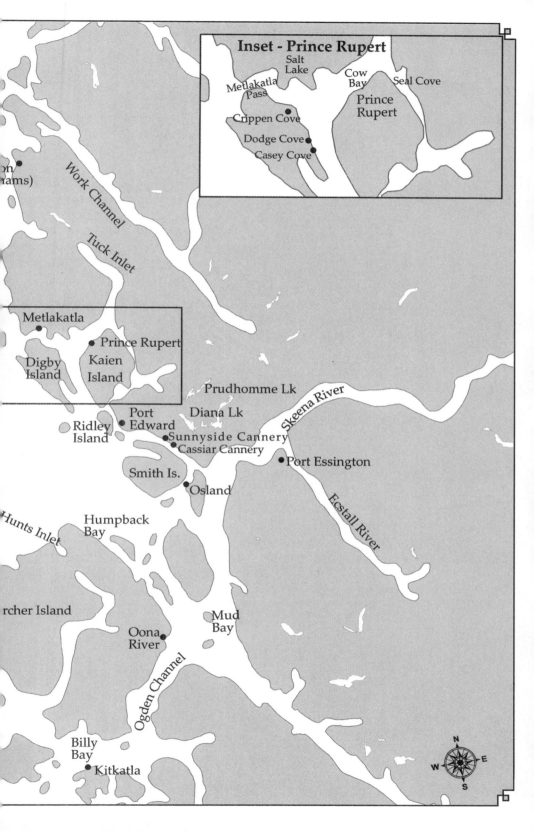

Inset - Prince Rupert

Salt Lake

Cow Bay

Seal Cove

Metlakatla Pass

Prince Rupert

Crippen Cove

Dodge Cove

Casey Cove

Work Channel

Tuck Inlet

Metlakatla

Prince Rupert

Digby Island

Kaien Island

Prudhomme Lk

Diana Lk

Skeena River

Ridley Island

Port Edward

Sunnyside Cannery

Cassiar Cannery

Port Essington

Smith Is.

Osland

Ecstall River

Hunts Inlet

Humpback Bay

rcher Island

Mud Bay

Oona River

Ogden Channel

Billy Bay

Kitkatla

N E S W

Home is a Tent

by Suellen Guenther

THINGS HAVE A WAY OF WORKING OUT. Those words have been my lifeline through many hard times. It took me a while to realize, however, that they seldom worked out the way I thought they would. My husband, Ed, and I immigrated to Canada in April 1970, following Ed's vision of dropping out of society and living an ecologically sound lifestyle. We were living in Barbados at the time, working as Peace Corps volunteers. In Canada, Ed hoped to avoid being drafted for the Vietnam War, as well as being able to homestead. Instead, back in the States awaiting our immigration papers to Canada, Ed was called up for his army physical. Miraculously, he failed. So when our papers arrived, we moved to Canada with no worries about the draft, only to find that homesteading in Canada had become a thing of the past. We also discovered that a lot of other people seemed to be dropping out of society and moving back to the land, seeking an alternative lifestyle. Since Ed had developed his ideas in relative isolation from North American society, this seemed especially strange to us.

When Ed first outlined his idea, I was less than enthusiastic. However, one of my deeply held beliefs is that each person in a marriage helps the other fulfill his or her dreams. Ed had joined the Peace Corps to support my dream, so now it was my turn to support his. The plan was to build a log house in the wilderness and live there for two years before getting on with the next part of our lives. It didn't work out that way, of course. It took us two years to *get* to the wilderness and five years to build the log house, where we lived for another seven years.

On our way to the wilderness, we camped around B.C. for three months in a pup tent, lived in Crippen Cove on Digby Island in a friend's cabin for a winter, lived on a boat tied to a dock in Prince Rupert while I taught school for a year, and spent three months as relief lightkeepers on Lucy Island light station with our six week-old son. It was an adventurous life for someone who had thought she would teach school in the same small town for years. It was exciting though, and we were still edging our way toward a dream that I had made my own.

One weekend, a friend from Prince Rupert took us out to Porcher Island to show us where he was born, and that's how we ended up in Oona River. Fortunately, one of the long-time residents there offered to sell us a few acres of his land, as members of the community were actively seeking young families to come and help keep their school open. We chose a lovely spot on his land about a half-hour hike through the muskeg from the community, on a little bay that we named Jade Cove.

However, when we applied to subdivide those 18 acres from the owner's 130, the land title office responded that it was a new subdivision and we would have to build a proper road from the community, two lanes wide, with culverts on each side. Now, aside from the fact that we couldn't afford to build such a road, it was the last thing we wanted. The whole idea was to live in the wilderness, bringing in our supplies by water. The site had the advantage of being near enough to a community of other people, but not so near that we had neighbours. The spot we had chosen was around a point from the village, out of sight, with no sign of other habitation in any direction. The landowner agreed to let us build on his land anyway, even though we didn't own it. We hoped a change at the land title office would eventually allow us to purchase it, with water access only. Near the end of our time there, this happened, and we did finally buy the land.

Anyone who has lived on the north coast of B.C. knows that it rains. A lot. Part of every day, if not all day, for most of the year. That made hiking through the muskeg to fall the trees for our log house a very cold, wet, unappealing proposition. After a few weeks of not much progress, we decided to put up a tent on the site and live there, so that Ed could come in out of the rain and warm up sometimes. The plan was to put up the tent and live in it for the summer, moving into our house in the fall.

What actually happened was that it took all summer to get the tent up and five years to build the house.

The tent was reasonably comfortable, with a wooden frame, door, and floor, a small, round, airtight wood stove for heating and cooking, and an old herring barrel for collecting rainwater. A copper boiler sat beside the stove to heat water for baths and laundry, and we used oil lamps for light.

Part of our plan was to live very simply, so we had no engines or power tools. We caught rides into Prince Rupert on fishing boats about every six weeks to get groceries, and then Ed rowed them around the point. He cut the trees for our house with a crosscut saw; each tree took a day to cut. I would come along, when I could, with our one year-old son, to limb and peel them. We burned beach logs for firewood, so the salt burned out our tin stove every six months and also ate away at the stovepipe.

Living the simple life had its challenges. I did laundry outside under a tarp on the driftwood front porch, using a washboard, plunger, and hand wringer. I would bring hot water from inside the tent for washing, and rinsed in cold rainwater, hauling buckets from the rain barrel to the wash-tub. It was dry there, but I usually did the wash wearing a jacket, toque and warm gloves inside rubber gloves. The wet laundry had to be hung in the tent to dry, so every few days we had wet diapers, clothes, and sheets slapping us in the face from clotheslines strung down the middle of the tent. When our second son came along, we had two in diapers. I ended up spending seven years washing diapers on a washboard.

Cooking on a tiny wood stove was another challenge. There was room on the top for a kettle to heat water or a frying pan, but not both, and I had to take them off to lift the lid and add more firewood. We ate a lot of one-pot skillet meals. However, with our first Christmas in the tent approaching, I also wanted to bake cookies. Ed looked at the design for a reflector oven in one of our back-to-the-land catalogues and then copied it, building a larger and much more useful one out of sheet metal. It was open on the side toward the stove, had a slanted top and bottom, and a shelf in the middle, so the heat from the side of the stove was captured and reflected onto the food on the shelf. The oven held a cookie sheet or two loaves of bread, which had to be turned to the heat every 10 minutes. Since I baked six loaves at a time, baking bread took most of the day. Occasionally I baked pies, mostly pumpkin, crowberry or salal berry, and I was secretly proud of the reputation I gained at community events when I produced a pie baked in that reflector oven.

Despite our goal of living off the land, we found we needed a certain amount of money. Our savings were dwindling, so Ed did various odd jobs, including a month working with a hand logger, helping the crew repair the gravel road in the community, digging a drainage ditch around the one-room schoolhouse, and working on fishing boats.

I was able to help when I was hired to teach school in the community the year I was pregnant with our second child. There were five students that year, from Grades 1-6. Since there were too few pupils to keep the school open, the children studied correspondence lessons sent from Victoria. The province paid a small amount per student and the parents paid a little as well. Although it wasn't a lot of money, it was a small monthly income.

Hiking across the muskeg in the winter was a particular challenge. It was dark when I left home and dark when I got back in those short, northern winter days. The time the batteries died in my flashlight was especially scary. It was a new moon, so there was very little light, and our trail was fairly rugged. I fell down a lot and had to feel my way, but I eventually made it home.

Then, over Christmas break, it snowed heavily and I had to break the

Suellen bakes bread in her reflector oven.

trail through the muskeg on my first hike back to work after the holiday, six months pregnant. It was exhausting. It continued to snow off and on that January, so sometimes I had to break the trail going across in the morning and again coming home at night. Usually snow didn't last very long in that climate – it would warm up and rain – but not that month.

Being pregnant in a tent had other challenges. Fitting into the round galvanized washtub to bathe was one. Lifting the buckets of water to do laundry was another. Living off the land meant we ate a lot of fish – fresh, canned, and salted – and we ate cod and turnip greens almost every day during the first three months I was pregnant, so even the smell of them cooking made me feel sick. Even now, just thinking about it makes me queasy. I haven't eaten turnip greens since.

Another challenge were the trips to the doctor in Prince Rupert for regular blood tests, as my blood type is RH negative. I was not brave enough to attempt a home delivery, especially with the risk that the baby would need a transfusion at birth, so I went to stay in Prince Rupert three weeks before my due date. Luckily, my baby was born 10 days early, so after staying in town for another week and then a week in Oona River, we brought our three week-old baby home to the tent.

However, as soon as I began lifting buckets of water to do laundry, I started to bleed. Ed radioed for a floatplane to come into the cove, and while several men from the sawmill came in their skiff to help carry my stretcher onto the plane, the sawmill caught fire. I felt terrible that they weren't there to help the community bucket brigade put out the fire, but there were acetylene tanks exploding high into the air, so maybe it was a good thing they didn't rush into the mill after all. Although I was terrified that I was bleeding to death, a simple procedure in hospital fixed the problem and I returned home.

Why did it take five years to build the house? The everlasting rain didn't help. Doing everything without power, including cutting firewood without a chainsaw, was painfully slow. It didn't help that Ed has suffered from bouts of depression for years. It was an enormous task for one person, and I am not a builder. We did have help twice. The men in the community came over and worked in teams to haul the logs out of the woods and stack them in a clearing above the house. Several years later, they came again to raise the rafters. A friend came to help Ed put the roofing material on, but otherwise, he built it alone. It was quite an achievement for a slight, intellectual man who was better at designing creative visions than implementing them.

After we moved into the house, things gradually became easier. We got a chainsaw to cut firewood, put a small outboard motor on our skiff, bought a propane cook stove with an oven, and set up a small gas generator. With power, we were able to run a small washing machine, and charge a battery system to light the house. One of my favourite memories is the wonder on our children's faces when Ed fired up the generator and we had shining lights on the Christmas tree for the first time.

Our original two-year vision became a lifestyle, and we stayed another seven years. However, gradually the dream house and beautiful natural setting began to feel like a trap. We had very little money and our boys were getting to the age where it would be difficult to get them to study by correspondence. Most men in that area found jobs in fishing or logging, and we wanted our sons to have other options. The endless grey skies and continual rain were depressing, and I came to dread waking up to the sound of rain dripping off the roof. You can imagine what the rain did to someone who suffers from depression.

So Ed applied to a masters program at the University of Victoria, and in 1985 we moved our family to the city. Adapting to city life was a culture shock, after living in the wilderness for 12 years. I found that all the

The finished product: the cabin at Jade Cove.

skills I needed to survive in the north were not needed in a city. Finding work was difficult, with 80 unemployed teachers in Victoria all vying for a few substitute teaching jobs, so our money was running out. The most painful adjustment for me was to find that a marriage that had withstood years of isolation in the Peace Corps and on the north coast did not survive living among people again.

I was 30 when we moved to Oona River and 42 when we left. I miss living in a setting surrounded by natural beauty in every direction, a place where I learned I am a survivor. I'm 70 now, and I still like to go camping for a few days every summer, with no electricity or running water. I like to hear leaves rustling and birds singing outside the tent and feel connected to nature and the whims of the weather again. And when I return home, I have a renewed appreciation for a comfortable bed, a hot shower, and a warm, dry place out of the weather. A little discomfort is good for me. And, in the end, things did have a way of working out, even though it wasn't the way I thought they would.

A Coastal Road

by Daphne Brown

IN 1974, NIXON RESIGNED and I came to Prince Rupert to meet up with my friend Pat. The previous spring, Pat and I hitchhiked to Berkeley, California from Vancouver and back, and made it through many adventures. Pat was the one who arrived first in Prince Rupert, looking for work, and I followed. We ended up sharing a cheap hotel room with thin walls and loud parties down the hall. We came for seasonal quick money, like many before us. Inexperience didn't worry us: a mishmash of dropouts and young and broke people were pouring into Rupert, buoyed by the feeling of a modern gold rush, if only we could catch it.

The fish canneries ran day and night: 12-hour shifts, as long as you could stand up. The aboriginal workers, who were skilled in this work, had an investment in this seasonal gold mine that many of us eventually came to understand. As time whipped by, we toughened up and learned to endure because the work was going to end soon.

At the start of each night we heard the slap of newly-caught salmon as they tumbled out of the chutes and poured down the production line in a gush of water, guts and blood. They were conveyed past rows of women covered from head to toe in rubber aprons and boots. Each person would grab as many fish as possible from the moving line to clean and scrape in an endless stream of flowing water. After 12 hours of hard work, we would pour into old school buses and roll home stinky and dirty. Heaven was a shower and fresh clothes. Heaven was sleep and good food, enough to keep you going for the next three months through this daily grind.

Paydays always gave us a rich feeling of reward. Working hard was good for the body and mind. Meeting new people and surviving the long nights with them felt like an accomplishment.

Then there was the rain. So much rain. We endured the endless weeks of work in a steady grey downpour. It was only when I was introduced to the harbour and islands surrounding Prince Rupert that water came to have a different meaning for me and I became part of the rainforest of the north coast.

I would sit on the dock outside the cannery and watch the boats line up for ice then cast off, headed for another salmon opening beyond the harbour. I began to wonder what was out there and who these people were, living a life of fuel docks and fish.

My first opportunity to find out about life beyond the harbour came early one morning. After a full night of work, all six of my cohorts and I set out on the water in a shaky old retired gillnetter to go crabbing, something I'd never done. The sun was out, and it was a fun adventure until the fog rolled in. Everything felt slowed down and it became hard to tell which direction we were headed. Through the blanket of fog, we inched forward to pick up the crab pots that we had set earlier in the day. When we finally had the last pot back on board, we limped our way back to the harbour feeling relieved to make it back safely to the dock. It had been frightening and exhilarating all at once. I was hooked.

Through the next few years I was able to test myself on the water again but under much better circumstances. After I had lived in a co-op house in Prince Rupert for about two years, I ended up living on a boat at the Fishermen's Co-op dock at Fairview for a year and a half. Then it was time to find a bigger space. I moved to Dodge Cove and, for two years, I helped

Crippen Cove in 1976.

caretake the house next to Norm's boat shed. My next stop was a cabin at Crippen Cove. This proved to be an invigorating and inexpensive lifestyle. Very gradually I weaned myself off the everyday conveniences of town life. Through this wonderful accident of time I came to belong to a boating community who fondly referred to themselves as water rats, and they became my lifelong friends. We had all followed similar paths to meet and explore a life by the waters off Prince Rupert away from what we had all previously considered the essential comforts of life.

Through the years, as the fishing fleet shrank and the jobs disappeared, many of us migrated south to Vancouver. One thread that holds us together is gathering and creating quilts in celebration of birth, life and death. These quilts now warm our beds and through each square remind us of the story of our friendships.

We don't all have skiffs, fishing boats or the space to mend nets, but we still congregate at the Blackberry Festival in Birch Bay. This is where the connection continues between the inhabitants of the north and south coast, then and now, along with many of the next generation. Friends gather from Prince Rupert to Vancouver, Nanaimo to Saskatchewan, and we all find a way to connect to that coastal northern rain forest town from our past: Prince Rupert.

It was girls like us who wanted to try everything. Whose parents weren't waiting around the corner to see if we were okay. Who weren't watching the first day we stepped into a leaky boat with virtual strangers. It was me

floating in a sea of fog, watching for familiar buildings to loom out of the fog and help me get my bearings.

A new quilt is unveiled in Vancouver, 2010.

A Prairie Chick on the Coast

by *Lorrie Thompson*

IN 1974, I WAS 19 years old when I left my home in Prince Albert, Saskatchewan and moved to Prince Rupert, British Columbia. I am the second youngest of a family of eight children, seven girls and one boy. I spent nearly 13 years in Prince Rupert and moved to Vancouver in 1987.

I had friends who had gone to Prince Rupert a year or so ahead of me and I heard through the grapevine that they had found work in the canneries. I didn't know more than that, but working in the canneries on the northwest coast of B.C. sounded very cool. And though I loved my family very much, I felt restless and in need of adventure. It was a big journey for me, leaving my prairie roots, and venturing out on my own, but hey man, it was the seventies.

I arrived in Prince Rupert in the autumn, during a rare sunny stretch of weather and it was truly spectacular! I fell in love instantly. This seaside fishing town at the end of the road gave me a very strong sense of freedom, partly because of my young age, and partly the times. The way of life rang true with me. Who would have thought that a prairie chick like me could feel such an affinity with the mountains and the sea? And it wasn't just the surroundings that gripped me but the people and hippie lifestyle. There were hundreds of young people coming from all over to work the herring and salmon seasons. There were jobs to be had and money to be made. Times were good. I soon made connections with the many people who still make up a large part of my strong and loving community.

I met Paul not long after I arrived, and lived with him at Salt Lakes for a few months. I remember our first romantic night together, crossing the harbour for my first time. It was a cold clear night, with snow on the ground and in the trees, a full moon, and a high tide. We took the skiff right up into the Salt Lake, something you can only do on a very high tide. It was beautiful.

I lived at Salt Lakes on and off (mostly on) for 10 years. It wasn't too long before Paul and I did the "Salt Lake Shuffle" (an endearing term used to describe the often changing relationships) and in 1977 I danced into the arms of Gene. We built a cabin together and had Linda Gibbs as a neighbour on one side and Margo and Hans Elfert on the other. It was a thrilling time, and Salt Lakes had a large and thriving community with about 10 occupied cabins.

The prevailing southeast winds blow right into Salt Lakes so many days were spent drinking coffee while watching the storms. Securing the boats at the dock and listening to C.B.C. radio went along with storm watching, as did quilting, spinning, knitting, mandolin playing, and keeping the fires burning. Sometimes I would find myself in my boat in one of the gales and though I was very rarely in danger it was often scary and always very wet. Having friends out on the water during a storm was worrisome and sometimes tragic. The power of the sea was something I learned early on to respect.

Hiking up the trail to the Salt Lake for a swim in the nude, and picking huckleberries along the way, were wonderful summer activities. Whether

Lorrie in Dodge Cove in the late-seventies.

it was copper-painting our wooden skiffs or canning sockeye salmon, work was usually done communally. Getting our firewood was one of my favourite chores. On a high tide we would go along the shoreline in our skiffs looking for the best logs for burning, and tow them to the beaches in front of our homes. Then on a low tide we would chainsaw and chop the wood and stack it in our wood sheds.

I have a vivid memory of a party in Salt Lakes on a lovely summer's evening, and a flotilla of boats arriving from Digby Island. We cooked salmon, abalone, shrimp, and crab on the beach and ate like royalty. I remember John saying, "I wonder what the rich are eating tonight?" We danced a lot that night too of course, and drank a punch that got more deadly as the night wore on. And I seem to remember a bit of an orgy happening in the back room. There were a couple of those over the years, like the Toga Party. I wasn't even there but I remember it well!

The morning after the beach party I had to work, and needless to say I was very hungover. I was working at Atlin Fish as the tally person, weighing the fishermen's catch, and I remember the boss gave me a shot of whisky to help me through the shift. On the way home that evening I noticed something floating in the middle of the harbour, and when I pulled up to it I realized it was the lid to our big pressure canner. The canner had been used the night before to cook shrimp, and the lid, forgotten on the beach, was carried away with the tide. I still use that canner every summer to can sockeye, a rewarding skill I acquired in my Prince Rupert days.

We used to go dancing often. The Ho Ho was one of our favourite dance spots in the basement of the Rupert Hotel. We would arrive *en masse*, strip off our many layers of backpacks, rain gear, and woollens, and pile them high in a corner. Then we would dance our hearts out! When the music stopped and the bar closed, we would gather up our clothing and head to one of the pizza joints. Finally at around 3 a.m. we would make our way back to the docks, climb into our skiffs and head home to Salt Lakes, Dodge Cove, or Crippen. If it was summer, it would be getting light and if winter, often stormy.

We had many wild and wonderful parties, and The Erotic Poetry Contests were no exception. A brainchild of Sebastian's, they were an annual event for two or three years. Sometime in spring we would rent one of the halls in town, put on our poets' costumes and our dancing shoes and have an entertaining night of fantastic poetry and dancing. The most memorable poem for me was when Linda Gibbs, Chloe Beam, Gene and I choreographed a dance to the Tina Turner song "Fire." In this case we did not put on our poets' costumes but took them off, and danced on the stage behind a sheet, creating a shadow dance. I heard it was pretty good.

I once went on a hand logging trip with Malcolm. He was in his early sixties when he built his 38-foot wood boat, the *Chilco*, in Dodge Cove. He had an order for a couple of mast poles and we must have travelled a fair distance as we were gone for a number of days. Being in a boat in the remote coastal inlets, completely surrounded by the natural world, is breathtaking. Once while we were boiling crab over a fire on the beach, a whale came up very nearby, awing us with its presence.

Malcolm lived to be 94, and in the last 20 years of his life he lived on his boat on Vancouver Island. Paul bought the *Chilco* from Malcolm a few years before he died and our daughter Elisha and her husband Theo spent many weekends with Malcolm learning what they could from him. They are now spending the summer on the *Chilco* with their new baby, Malcolm.

In the early seventies, a group of friends, including Paul, bought a remote piece of property on Porcher Island. I was not in the initial group but became involved later. Porcher Island is 25 kilometres southwest of Prince Rupert and the property is up Serpentine Inlet with a protected anchorage. A one-kilometre hike across the muskeg lies Oval Bay, an isolated five-kilometre stretch of beach, completely exposed to the ferocious southeast gales.

One winter I spent Christmas there with a large group, six adults and five children. It happened to be a cold spell with no snow, and the muskeg had frozen. Perfect conditions for ice skating. Richard and Paul, in their great wisdom, had collected a few pairs of second-hand skates and on Christmas Day we all skated for hours. The older kids had their dog attached to a sled to pull the younger ones. We covered ground that was next to impossible to traverse when not frozen, and because it was so shallow there was no risk of the ice breaking and falling in. Every now and then the ice would shift and there would be a thunderous noise echoing across the sky. Magical indeed.

In early summer one year Paul, Ghislaine and I took two skiff loads of garden supplies to Serpentine. A large area in the muskeg was being turned into fertile garden soil. We spent a number of days hauling up wheelbarrow loads full of lime, fish meal and seaweed to the garden. One of my favourite things to do there was to bathe in the old cast iron claw-footed bathtub set up outside a small creek. We would fill the tub with water from the creek, light a fire under it and keep it going for a few hours. Then at the end of a hard day's work, we'd relax in a hot bath. A room with a view, indeed.

The garden at Serpentine Inlet.

I made the trip back to Prince Rupert by myself, leaving Serpentine a few days after Ghislaine and Paul. I left in the evening with the tide and travelled a couple of hours to Billy Bay where Barb was living. I spent the night at Billy Bay and left with the tide early the next morning. It was a long 10 hour trip in an open skiff, and I felt very independent.

Paul and I got back together in 1983 and in 1985 we had our first child Elisha. We bought Bill and Shelley's house in Crippen Cove and moved there when Elisha was six months old. We only lived a couple of years in Crippen Cove but, like Salt Lakes, the lifestyle was unique and challenging.

The tides in Prince Rupert are quite extreme, with more than 20 feet between the high and the low. At Crippen you don't do anything without checking the tide table. At high tide you can have the ocean lapping at your doorstep and at low tide it can hardly be seen. Getting stranded at low tide, losing a gumboot in the quicksand mud, or hauling your supplies and children up the mud flats were daily occurrences and hard work.

The community was strong and supportive and in many ways an ideal place to raise a family, but Elisha was only 2½ when we left Crippen Cove and the north coast and moved to Vancouver. We were in pursuit of jobs, a sunnier climate, a new adventure. We still own the house in Crippen Cove, and in the mid-nineties, Paul, Elisha, our two year-old son Ezra, a friend Mark and I drove up to Rupert, and re-roofed the house. That was the last time I was in Prince Rupert.

Thinking back on my time in Prince Rupert, I can only feel grateful for the many unique and fascinating experiences I had. It was a risky lifestyle but I'm happy I took the risks and braved the storms. I'm thankful for the friends I made, and for the strong community we've built and maintained. Helen Keller once said, "life is either a daring adventure or nothing. Security does not exist in nature, nor do the children of men experience it. Avoiding danger is no safer in the long run than exposure."

I would like to dedicate this memoir to my mother and father and my seven siblings who taught me about the importance and beauty of a strong community. And to my children and my children's children who are my biggest adventure of all.

The gang at Salt Lakes.

Gardens on the Edge

by Nancy Fischer

IT WAS RUPERTING SIDEWISE all day long a few days ago in North Cove on Washington's south coast, so we spent the day doing inside chores. In the afternoon it let up enough that my husband, Steve, decided to go out and check on the flock. As he walked down the driveway toward the coops, the biggest eagle he had ever seen lifted from the field, followed by two huge ravens. In the field he discovered poor Einstein's head, a foot and a few feathers. Alfreda E. Einstein had been a friendly egg-laying golden Indian runner duck. The last time I lost a pet to aerial predation was nearly four decades ago in a cove named after Lionel Crippen on an island off British Columbia's north coast.

I only had one bird then, a chicken who was my dog MacInTOSH Rock Mudball Extraordinaire's best buddy. Although he'd been punished for killing chickens while living on Anian Island, he never bothered this one, and, in fact, saved her life. He jumped and barked like never before until we saw his chicken in the mouth of a visiting puppy. So when I came home from school to find the chicken gone, I never suspected him, especially since there was a skiff of snow on the ground and not one trace of blood. It must have been an eagle.

My former husband, Terry, and I hitchhiked to P.R. from Seattle over Christmas vacation in 1973. In Prince Rupert we were both offered jobs, so the following summer we immigrated. On a beautiful turquoise day during our first winter we paddled our canoe to Crippen Cove on Digby Island to visit the local health food store owner, Geof. Leaving that evening, we noticed one house was still in the sunlight. A wind came up and our canoe swamped, so we paddled our drenched selves back to the Cove and dried our clothes by Geof and Sheila's tin heater before Geof towed the canoe back to town behind *Put-Put*, his single cylindered Easthope driven runabout. A couple of months later we bought that house in the sun. Now we commuted daily to our jobs over this same stretch of water roiled by North Pacific winds and strong tidal currents.

At first we either paddled to town, or caught the ferry that brought the workers from Rupert to the airport on Digby. One morning a boat was perched on a rock near the entrance to Crippen Cove. Richard, her owner, reclined in the sloping companionway, smoking a cigarette, calmly reading a book of poetry as he waited for the tide to float his *Nora Flynn*. A few weeks later he gave us a 14-foot riveted aluminum skiff called the *Silver Bitch* that seemed much safer than the canoe for harbour crossing. She leaked so badly that it took four lines to keep her afloat while we were at work: she'd fill with water but the motor didn't quite submerge. We'd bail and head across the harbour in our new boat.

But crossing the harbour was only one aspect of that young life on the other side. The back-to-the-land self-sufficient lifestyle of wood heat, outhouses, kerosene lamps, huge gardens and rainwater catchment systems was quite comfortable, as I also worked a full-time teaching job in town too, with the effortlessness of youth.

When we moved to our yellow and blue house in the sun, it had an old rotten white enamel cook stove and a tin heater. The stovepipes pierced the ceiling and then joined to go through the roof, which showed signs of previous chimney fires that miraculously hadn't burned down the whole shebang. I procured a half-sized steel floor wax drum from the school custodian and drew a design like the tin heater. It had a rolled steel liner, stainless steel hinges on the top and a damper on the front. For $40, Rupert Sheet Metal in Cow Bay altered my barrel and I had a steel tin heater that survived 20 years of burning salt wood. Once the coals were good, that heater would hold a fire all night on two half-rounds of hemlock and by opening the damper in the morning a pot of water would boil in no time. In summer, one cardboard box sent roaring up the chimney would take off the morning chill. Twice I had one of the sheet metal companies in Rupert fashion new linings for the old cook stove and it too lasted another 20 years, although I used the cook stove only for baking, preserving food or flapjacking, not for heat.

Almost immediately, we began turning over the west front yard for a garden. The east side had the remnants of a garden and great black currant bushes. I discovered the tenacity of buttercup (*Ranunculus*) and my ex's sedentary tendencies. I tried turning the soil, piling it,

Nancy examines a crab pot on the beach of Crippen Cove.

and covering it with black plastic, but the buttercups had to be completely dug out. My neighbour, Sheila, actually named her boat *Buttercup* and painted it yellow because she believed this would ensure safe harbour crossing. One night we were the only ones at home in the Cove; it was blowing a gale. About midnight a knock came on our door. There stood Geof, drenched after sailing *Buttercup* across the harbour alone. The light from our kerosene lamps had beckoned him.

The garden provided loads of food. Each fall I would pack five-gallon buckets of seaweed up the path from the beach and spread it on the garden. I always admired Dolly's ability to pack four buckets at a time, two in each hand. How quickly she could mulch her garden! We raked brown popweed off the nearby beaches, piled it into the canoe or *Silver Bitch*, and took it back to Crippen and up the hill. It always took me several days, with Tosh tagging along. I swore I'd put a backpack on him, but never did. This and the fish meal that I swept off the floor of the Fishermen's Co-op made the black muck soil very rich. No lime was needed because just two feet down was solid midden which more than once bequeathed bone awls, beaver and dog teeth, and ancient stone scrapers to the garden above.

Corn was planted through plastic sheets that warmed the soil. The tomatoes and peppers, and even okra, were planted under old wood-framed lattice windows that were hinged with shoe leather across a sawhorse-like structure. Once all my corn was blown down by the down-draft of a helicopter, as someone from town landed on Harding's Point where Bill and Shelley lived. Seaplanes often flew over. The gardens at Crippen were weeded occasionally by barebacked hippie chicks and the pilots knew it! They missed the time Chloe, a couple of other girls, and I decided to sunbathe on the dock with nothing but zucchini and crook neck squash flowers for fig leaves. Ember, Chloe's man, came home and ran up to the house without a sideways glance or a word.

Apples grew in the cove, if the deer allowed. One time I planted a new tree with a few fish heads for fertilizer, and the next day it was dug up. Wolf poop proclaimed the culprits. Placing boards atop the ground kept them from repeating their rummaging. These skinny mangy wolves subsisted on barnacles and people's pets. Bill and Shelley rushed their dog Barney to the vet in town after a wolf performed a tracheotomy on him. He lived, but could never tell the tale. Dolly and Alan told me they watched Tosh resist the lure of a wolf at the edge of the forest behind their house. Tosh was a survivor.

We grew flowers too. I used "Hollyhock Hill" as a call-sign on the battery powered C.B. radio. We had poppies all along the center walkway that I later learned gave us hippies a bad reputation. They were Malvern Giants: *Papaver orientalis*, nothing like *P. somniferans*, the opium poppies of Afghanistan. They were far more beautiful, and so were the Himalayan blue poppies *Meconopsis*. There were wild roses covering the hill on the water side, and I once considered blindsiding my neighbour when he pulled up my rose starts along the fence between our properties (he was ornery and eventually was shot dead by someone up in the Northwest Territories). In the woods behind the house grew a patch of wild coral-root orchids (*Corollorhiza*) and carnivorous sundews (*Drosera*) and deer ferns (*Blechnum*). In fact, my love affair with the watery native muskeg plants actually precipitated the end of my sojourn in the north. My reason for leaving was to study with a professor who was the native plant guru at the University of Washington in Seattle.

The gardens of Crippen Cove never wanted for water, but the house did. The rainwater catchment system consisted of wooden gutters connected by various lengths of hose funnelled into whiskey barrels under the house, and galley pump at the kitchen sink. We had an outhouse, which I replaced with an A-frame squatter. It was back behind the house in the woods and was only slightly difficult in the middle of the night when it was pouring rain. Terry's parents came to visit once, and after slipping off the two logs that we called our dock, his father dropped his wallet down the squatter. They didn't visit again. For showers I'd heat a canner of water and use a saucepan for a dipper outside. I always felt clean, but learned, years later, that some people used to think I stunk! They didn't like the wood smoke smell that permeated my existence in those days.

The smokehouse was even further back in the woods. This mossy relic looked as though it had been there since the house was built in 1927. It was outfitted with racks for fish and screens for clams and had a hole near the bottom to which I attached a stovepipe, leading to an old tin heater. Salmon were plentiful in the latter half of the seventies, as we now had a diesel-powered St. Pierre Dory and could easily catch all the fish we needed, some for smoking, some for canning. Sometimes a couple or three of us girls would get together and do a group canning on one of our wood cook stoves using two or three canners. It was usually an all-night proposition. Sometimes it would get so hot that we'd take off some of our clothes. It's a wonder that we didn't get injured by all those hot jars, steam, and fire. Everything had to be canned in those days, but everyone had an All American pressure canner and we were experts at all kinds of preserving.

We even made our own alcoholic beverages. I would make about 10 gallons of black currant wine each year. It was a good red and years later when I brought some to a dinner party in Seattle, the host, a Ph.D. biochemist, proclaimed that it tasted just like his grandfather's wine in Italy. I doubted that, but I accepted the compliment. I used to make beer too. From Northern Drugs I could get a can of hop-flavoured malt extract for $5. Combined with some yeast and sugar, it produced a passable beer, in spite of being brewed behind the stove

"Everything had to be canned in those days."

in a semi-sterile plastic bucket. Dolly made an excellent ginger beer. Chloe made great wine from her huge patch of raspberries. And one year Shelley made real grape wine using a press that Bill built. I also made dandelion wine, which required painstakingly separating the petals of the dandelion flowers and combining them with oranges, lemons, raisins and yeast sprinkled on rye toast. It took seven years to become quite like brandy in colour and flavour, but not much of it made it to that degree of maturity. I still have a quilted pillow that Kristen Miller traded me for wine.

Kerosene lamps provided light, although battery-powered C.B.s were common. One night, after I knocked over a lit lamp, kerosene spread across the floor, but the fire licked up and out, and I was able to scoop the lit wick safely into the sink. Matches were laid out beside the lamp so that we could find them in the morning darkness. The ides of March was the day that the lamps didn't have to be lit before going to work. Spring at last! With no phones, I knew the power was out in town (which cancelled school and a harbour crossing) if the hospital was the only building in town with lights. Bill and Shelley had a T.V. that ran on a car battery and we'd all crowd their living room to watch *Dallas*. Bill built a mute button by attaching a toggle switch to the T.V. speaker wire.

As the seventies ended, rural electrification came to Crippen Cove. By now I was on my own, and the opportunity to modernize was irresistible. I drew up a plan, took it to the electrical inspector in Prince Rupert and began wiring the house. It was a simple 20-by-20-foot house, two rooms, a pantry and attic. By kerosene lamp, I'd wire the outlets and switches. In the day I'd run wire underneath and drill up through ancient hemlock timbers using a neighbour's generator to power the drill. Attaching the lights, switches and outlets was easy. The incredulous inspector approved this girl's wiring job. The whole thing cost me $300. I earned that back by helping burn the slash from clearing for the helicopter-planted power poles. When a 750-gallon herring tote floated in, I hauled it up the hill, set it on a grid of timbers, attached a plastic pipe and spigot and all of a sudden I not only had electricity, but running water too.

For three years I commuted across the harbour to teach school. I thought I was in heaven walking the beach or scrambling the bog lantern-lit trail before school on clear days. I'd ride the airport ferry or take our dory from the Cove to town. But the sequel to the fairy tale is a story of wild nightmarish weather, deadheads, icy docks, engines that only half worked, frozen fingers, fog, and dead friends. People died when they were crossing the harbour or fishing. I still can't sleep if the wind blows, as I can't help remembering bucking boats breaking their moorings and wreckage on rocks. I left in 1983, but continued to return several times a year until I sold the place in 1993.

I have fewer teeth and more grey hair, and my hands don't work very well, but I still jar salmon. My smoked clams are now razors instead of butter. I still live by the sea, in Washington state, with a brilliant gardener/carpenter in a magical space. The same black currants and Venn Passage spearmint, smuggled over the border, are growing by my pond and the same gorgeous poppies line my walkways. I make blackberry mead from Linda Gibbs' blackberries. Linda's husband John has encouraged us to add poultry to our place. I haven't been back across the harbour to Crippen, but I keep in touch with most of the gang at weddings and birthdays and always at the annual Blackberry Jamboree. The semi self-sufficient lifestyle is still alive and well. My beloved pal Tosh is laid to rest near the foundation of a house that my dad built. Tsunami, a.k.a. Tsuzie the cat, has coyotes instead of wolves to watch out for and we help our chickens and ducks evade eagles and mink. They help us joyfully proclaim that life is wonderful in our garden on the edge.

Some Gumboot Girls show off their footwear at the 2012 Blackberry Jamboree.

Into the Abyss

by Carol Manning

FATE BROUGHT ME HERE.
Fate, and that restless searching
The feeling there had to be more.
The universal search
For meaning.
I say yes to gut feelings.

Impulsively stepping into the unknown,
Quit my government job.
Go West.
Via Rail to Edmonton
Bicycle to Jasper, to Lake Louise, on to Vancouver.
Did I mention I'd never seen a mountain?
There was no turning back.

Fateful friendship...fateful love.
Searching.
The creative wave that caught the light
Of my interest,
My direction,
Ripples still.

Needing the grounding of routine,
A sense of purpose.
Looking for work
In a nameless building.
Leafing through a countertop catalogue while waiting for assistance.
A catchy phrase sent me to another building,
To the office of an anonymous person, who had just received a call,
From someone searching for an employee.
A job opening.
Qualifications matched.
Off to Prince Rupert.

Stepping into the unknown,
Eagle flew past the bus, guiding me to town.
Fate and Raven's curiosity keep me here.
Like others, I came for two years and stayed a lifetime.

Living on the fringe,
Between the intensity of work
And the energy of the city, pulsing with seasonal fishing cycles,
Surrounded by wild beauty.
It was the best of times: stability, certainty, contentment,
Grounded and supported in a challenging routine.
From my students I learned
To cook chow mein buns like the Pagoda made,
And so much more.

Hiked
The Chilkoot, Haida Gwaii, Hudson Bay
  Mountain.
Trying to balance
Work and play
Missed the mark — work won.

*On the Chilkoot
Trail, 1981.*

On the fringe of a fluid community
That inspired, and broadened my awareness.
Adventurous, capable people manifesting their dreams.
From outlying areas they
Passed through the Museum of Northern B.C.
Connected through C.B.C.'s message time
Ordered with the Slack Tide Food Co-op.

On the fringe of creativity.
Hues Gallery in an empty apartment over a store on 3rd Ave.
Photographers caught by the northern light, striving to find the definitive
  image.
Erotic Poetry Contests between halibut and salmon openings.
Artists, together, raised the pole at the Museum carving shed.
Carvers taught me to sharpen my kitchen knives on a whetstone.

On the fringe of political-social movements.
People joined to establish the Transition House
People worked with S.O.S. – Save Our Shores from the first Kitimat
  pipeline proposal.

> *We had dreams when the night was young*
> *We were believers when the night was young*
> *We could change the world, stop the war.*
> *Never seen nothing like this before.*
> *~Robbie Robertson, "When the Night Was Young"*

But
Friends move
Love drifts
Circumstances change
Fate intervenes.

Stepping into the unkown again.
Lost was absolute thinking
Gained were shades of grey.

Then the quilters,
Working together to honour life's events:
The arrivals, the departures, and the messiness in between.
The quilters, my Sisters of Mercy, my lifeline when all was flux
Who tended my uncertainties.
Who encouraged my expression
An amoebic group with far reaching pseudopods
Enfolding a changing collection of people.
Unexpected, casual friendships evolved into
A caring, accepting, interesting community.

Now, the intuition that found so many connections continues.
Stepping into the unknown is no longer as dramatic.
I can stand in the chaos as winds of change swirl around me.
Always the dance with fear.
Fear the restrictor…fear the protector.

Eagle now sits outside my house.
Raven's magic still intrigues me.
I appreciate all that is the abyss of life.

> *I was so much older then*
> *I'm younger than that now.*
> ~Bob Dylan, "My Back Pages"

The Test of Time

by Dolly Harasym

THE YEAR WAS 1974. I was living on Cortes Island, broken-hearted and jobless. I felt the need to leave the island to find employment and reflect on my next direction. There was much debate amongst my friends about where the best opportunities were for work, and Prince Rupert with its numerous fish processing plants seemed the best option. My friend Annie wanted to join me, so we headed north on B.C. Ferries to a city we knew absolutely nothing about.

My first impression of Prince Rupert, as Annie and I walked into town from the ferry dock, was how wild and isolated this place was. There was no sign of life until we reached the Totem Lodge. The road was forested on either side and eerily quiet except for the ravens cawing at us from the trees.

Once we reached the downtown core my impression changed. The city was alive and bustling. After putting in resumés at several businesses, Annie found work at the Totem Lodge as a night desk clerk and I was hired on at the co-op cannery. Fortune was not on my side though, because after working only a couple of days the plant had a lockout. By the time the dispute ended there were only a few days of work left before us new hires were laid off.

Annie saved a little money and returned to Cortes Island in the fall, but I stayed to look for other employment. I waitressed in the dining room at the old Rupert Hotel, and then worked in the hotel bar after I turned 19. I somewhat enjoyed living and working in the city, but was lonely and homesick for the back-to-the-land lifestyle I had left behind on Cortes and the people I knew there. I wasn't really cut out to be a barmaid and was contemplating looking for a different job once the fish plants got going again. One evening I received a phone call at home from a fellow employee to tell me not to bother going into work that evening because the hotel had burned down.

I went back to work at various fish plants popping herring roe and filleting ground fish. There was never a problem finding a job in those days. You could walk into almost any business and be hired on the spot. Eventually I found steady work at the Seal Cove cold storage plant where groundfish were processed and frozen. Numerous draggers fished out of Prince Rupert at that time, and when they came in to unload there would be huge mounds of sole and rockfish piled up on the floor for us plant workers to process. The bigger the pile, the happier we were, because it meant overtime and a fat paycheque.

This was an exciting time period in Prince Rupert with fishermen and cannery workers arriving in droves for the fishing season. At times the boats would be rafted up at the dock six or more abreast, and the harbour would be lit up like a city from boats at anchor. It was a time for working hard, partying lots, and just living the moment.

It was during this time period that some of my longest lasting friendships were forged. None of us realized that this city, the northern lifestyle and our friendships would grow on us, so we all stayed longer then planned.

It was also a time when people wanted to live on the land, on the fringes of society, and become somewhat self-sufficient. There was a migration from the city to places like Salt Lake, Crippen Cove, Dodge Cove, Anian Island, Skiakl Bay, Billy Bay, Simms Bay, Serpentine Inlet, and Humpback Bay. Someone purchased the inland ghost town of Pacific, a place only accessible by train. The new owner of the town advertised in papers all over North America to interest people in buying into the place to start a new community. He also organized the first Pacific reunion so that people could come and check the place out, enjoy a weekend of music, and hopefully buy a share in the town. It was more fun riding the train out to Pacific than the actual event itself. People on their way to the reunion flagged the train down in the most obscure places. Many of us had instruments. The conductor left his radio turned on so the engineer could be entertained by the jam session, and listen to me play a jig on my fiddle.

I became involved in an environmental group, S.O.S. (Save Our Shores), a group of people dedicated to stopping the proposed building of the Mackenzie Valley pipeline and ensuing tanker traffic. It was a threat to the fishing industry that so many of us depended on, as well as to the diverse marine life and the way of life of northern and coastal peoples. Sometimes our meetings would carry on into the bar, and it was on one of these occasions that my friend Shelley Lobel introduced me to a fisherman named Alan. He had spent the winter in Queen Charlotte

Dolly plays a tune on her fiddle.

City on his boat, was lonely, and had come to Prince Rupert because he knew that there would be an influx of women arriving for the herring season. Alan and I continued to see each other between his fishing trips on the *Anthony J*, a seine and halibut boat that he worked on. My plans for moving back to Cortes Island were soon forgotten. I had a new man in my life, a great network of friends, and a job that I really enjoyed.

Perhaps because of my prairie upbringing and a history of farming on both sides of my family, I had a real interest in the back-to-the-land lifestyle. I grew up with gardening and preserving food for the winter, so the back-to-the-land movement was not as new to me as it was to city people looking for a new way of life.

I was interested in buying into the co-operatively owned Serpentine property on Porcher Island, but after making the trip out to the inlet with Alan and Richard, one of the shareholders, I could see that it would be a tough and lonely place to live. I was impressed, though, with the garden that Richard had carved out of the raw land.

In 1977, Alan and I decided to make our relationship permanent. He didn't want to live in town so we checked out a couple of properties that were for sale in Kelp Pass and Hunts Inlet. One had already sold and the other was too remote. Alan heard of a place across the harbour in Crippen Cove on Digby Island that we could caretake. I had my own boat with an inboard motor at the time so I ventured over at high tide to check the place out, a 2 ½ mile ride from the closest point in town. I was not at all impressed with the house. It was just a tiny rundown shack built during the depression, but there was a small community of people living in the cove so at least there would be neighbours. One of those people was Nancy Fischer, who made a huge impression on me with her abilities and skills.

With a promise from Alan that the shack could be fixed up, I agreed to move to Crippen Cove. It was a tough adjustment for me at first. I felt like I had lost my independence when I gave up my job at the fish plant to move to this semi-isolated community, but over the years I would gain a new kind of independence, one that comes with meeting the challenges of island living. I was not used to having a large body of water, weather and tides dictating my comings and goings. The Cove didn't have a government dock so boats had to be moored out or tied to clotheslines attached to land at one end and a float at the other. When the tide went out, the boats would dry up on the mud flat, making commuting difficult. Grocery shopping and laundry days in town had to be well planned. Many of the people I knew were a boat ride away, making us a community of friends living our lives separated by water. A visit was a pleasant outing when summer days were long and seas calm, but we might just as well have been miles apart during the dark and stormy days of winter.

Dolly reels in a boat on a clothesline in Crippen Cove.

Sometimes all of us women just wanted to have a break from our alternative lifestyle, so we'd head off to town in our boats, gumboots, and rain gear for a women's night out of dancing at one of the many night clubs.

We didn't have electricity, telephones, cell phones or Internet in those early days, so in order to get word out to friends living remotely, messages could be sent through message time on C.B.C. radio. This was a vital link for many people.

The first year that I lived in the Cove, I tried my hand at commercial crab fishing and ventured out for day trips in Chatham Sound, but it was miserable working out of the herring punt with no protection from the elements. Because I was in a new relationship, I didn't like spending so much time by myself so I gave up crab fishing.

In 1978 I worked on a dig with a group of archaeologists on Ridley Island before the coal and grain terminals were built there. I also provided boat transportation, a job that I took over from Alan when he left for down south to look for a fishing boat to purchase.

In 1979 I started my fishing career with Alan on our new 36-foot troller, the *Nowthen*. That was the big herring year. It was like the Wild West out on the fishing grounds with the price reaching unheard-of levels. Fishermen raced up and down the coast to catch every opening. They sold their catch for cash and carried around wads of money. We pretty well paid off the boat that season. I put in part of the salmon season off the west coast of Haida Gwaii, but had to pack it in early because I was pregnant and started having complications.

Life in the Cove became easier as time went on. B.C. Hydro hooked the community up to the power grid in 1980. More people moved to Crippen and Dodge Cove and started their own families. Alan and I had a second child in 1982. Our children grew up with lots of freedom, but always under the watchful eyes of the whole community. When they were of school age they had to be taxied by skiff to the airport dock to catch the Metlakatla school ferry to attend school in Prince Rupert. This was a task usually taken on by the women in Crippen Cove.

It was somewhere around 1982 that Kristin Miller, a good friend and avid quilter who lived in Salt Lake, became a huge influence to all of the women in the island communities. Under her guidance we started making medallion-style quilts as a collective effort. It wasn't always possible for us to get together because of our separation by water, so a quilt top would be passed around from person to person so that everyone involved could add her round at her own convenience. Over the years we ended up making many quilts in this tradition for births, deaths, weddings and illnesses. There has never been any plan to our quilt making, so no one knew how it would turn out until after the last person worked on it. The quilt in progress would travel by boat from community to community, usually protected in a garbage bag from rain and sea spray. On one occasion a quilt was accidentally thrown into the dumpster at the dock by a husband who got the trash and quilt bags mixed up. Fortunately he was able to retrieve it before the garbage was picked up.

In the winter of 1984 Alan and I did a very bold thing: we took a job with Canadian University Services Overseas, uprooted our two boys, and moved to Vanuatu in the South Pacific where Alan was to teach fishing techniques to villagers. His knowledge of fishing and our lifestyle made us perfect candidates for the job that would see us living overseas for almost 2½ years on a small remote island. We would travel by boat into other remote island communities where Alan would teach his courses, and I would teach the women how to sew and bake bread in their bush ovens. We returned to Canada in the spring of 1987 and resumed our lives amongst our friends. By that time the dynamics of our coastal communities were changing. Some of the women moved south to further their careers or find new opportunities, while others moved closer to town. Families were growing and community events were geared more towards the children.

The one constant in our ever-changing busy lives was quilting. I had missed out on participating in several group quilts when I was overseas, but more were in the works. We would gather at the Dodge Cove schoolhouse, or up at C.B.C. hill house. One day my wonderful friends surprised me with a beautiful garden quilt they had made for me. Each square represented an aspect of the beauty of a garden.

With both of my boys in school, I really wanted to have some sort of a career. I decided to run a business from home doing something I loved. We installed two permanent greenhouses, and I grew bedding and vegetable plants, and made hanging baskets that I sold through a hardware store in Prince Rupert.

In 1995 we moved into Prince Rupert so the boys could have a better social life while finishing up high school. Over the years I had spent many hours taxiing them back and forth across the harbour for after-school activities, or just to be with their friends. I wasn't going to miss commuting in the fog or foul weather, especially in the dark of winter when you could hear the wind howling across the harbour but you couldn't see how bad it really was. There had been a few times that I had to knock on a friend's door in town to ask if the boys and I could spend the night. The sad part about moving into town was that we hadn't quite finished renovating our new house. It was a purchase made from Jimmy, a real pioneer in his day. It was built years ago at his mill up the Ecstall River. The house was skidded onto a huge float and towed to Crippen Cove where it was placed on new pilings.

Life in town had its advantages. I upgraded my education at the college and honed my sewing skills at courses. I became a businesswoman for a time when Alan and I moved our fish market from the *Porcher G*, a boat at the dock, to a building in Cow Bay. I opened a small restaurant, fish market and fish processing business that is still in operation bearing my name, though I no longer own it.

I think that all of us women have been caught up with busy schedules between work and families, so the opportunities to visit are fewer. The one way that we have stayed connected is through our quilting. Now our quilts travel by mail as well as by boat. We gather in cyberspace and stay in communication via e-mail.

When I reflect on my journey to Prince Rupert in the seventies and the ensuing years, I have to say that life in this northern coastal community has been opportunistic, challenging, fun and character-building. That was our time, a place in history like no other. Even though there were bumps along the way, I wouldn't change it for the world. I cherish the family that I have and the friendships that I've made that have stood the test of time.

North Coast Fashions

by Shelley Lobel

I WAS RAISED IN A JEWISH middle class home by a dad who was a clothing manufacturer and a mom who later in life became an interior decorator. My mom was a stunning dresser, always turning heads with her latest couture fashion. As a child, I would gush with pride whenever she dressed up, which was every day, and asked, "How do I look?" Her vanity kept her looking spectacular into old age and she maintained that movie star look even through the ravages of Alzheimer's.

My Dad, a charming showoff, was a great guy but appearances were supremely important to him. His wife was deeply in love with him, always responsive to his every wish. She was a martyr. Although the dynamics of their relationship were not unusual in that time, it was difficult to watch.

"Syl, you don't have enough lipstick on" was a recurring refrain in our house. He wanted his daughters to be like her, perfect and elegant. "Shelley, stand up straight, stomach in, comb your hair." First impressions count: that was his motto.

Growing up with a dad who had a clothing factory should be every girl's dream. My sister and I were allowed and encouraged to choose whatever we wanted from racks and racks of clothing. Even though I was privileged, I wasn't aware of it, and even as a young child I began to rebel. I didn't want to dress up, go out for dinner, or even go shopping with my mom. I never had a Sweet Sixteen, a huge coming-of-age event, where all my friends would attend an expensive party and everyone would try to outdo one another. My clearest memory of that time was wearing a stunning green silk gown and being so nervous that my sweat created huge rings around my armpits, reaching towards my breasts. Everything was a huge hassle, especially anything my parents expected of me.

What kind of life was that? When I met Bill, who had hitchhiked across Canada to Penticton, I quickly got my hair coiffed and squeezed into a cute outfit to make a lasting impression on him. I did, and that was the beginning of huge changes that fostered my independence and a new way of life. I left for a two-week vacation in B.C. and stayed for 40 years.

In the first year together, we tried making a living in the Okanagan picking fruit, and even received a Local Initiative Project (L.I.P.) grant. The local economy was dead, so we headed off to Victoria (which was just as bad) and then a friend encouraged us to go north to Prince Rupert.

Prince Rupert felt like a perfect fit for us: jobs, affordable housing, friendly people, eye-popping scenery, and fresh air. After a month of settling in, we met up with a very charismatic fellow who introduced us to the harbour by taking us to Crippen Cove on Digby Island one starry evening by skiff. You can only imagine six strangers, who recently met at the local bar, crammed into a large wooden skiff, putting along while transfixed by the sunset and the choppy waves. When the boat came to an abrupt halt, to our amazement, John informed us that the tide was going out and we were in shallow water on the mudflats of Crippen Cove. To this day I remember my reaction when John commanded, "Everyone out." No one had boots or any understanding about tides. Wading through the icy water and feeling the muck grabbing onto my feet was my initiation with the way I was going to live for the next 10 years of my life.

When the opportunity to care-take a cottage in the Cove came up, we grabbed it. This property made me feel special, with its small yellow clapboard house on a point and green lawn stretching to the water. The long forgotten Jewish princess had arrived in her new home! It was rustic but picturesque: the lack of running water, electricity, or flushing toilet didn't bother me. The crappy weather didn't bother me; nothing mattered: we were young, in love and full of adventure. We got a boat and a motor and began our new life.

My dad never did come to visit. The outhouse would have finished him for sure! My mom, bless her, did. She just wanted to see me and perhaps this trip would put her at ease. She arrived in a private jet, having hitched a ride with one of her wealthy clients. We whisked her off in a small open boat to our magical island. I was so thrilled by her arrival, I had completely forgotten that she didn't know how to swim and was truly terrified of the water. Of course, she'd sleep in the master bedroom with its million-dollar view and naturally she was given a chamber pot just in case. I still can picture her using our hand-built outhouse, which I thought was a work of art and one of the best features of the property. My mom, ever the martyr, never said a word.

In that week, we made the obligatory trip to town. The weather had changed to being windy and damp and I was fearful for her fragility. Here's where my sense of reality, my sense of fashion, and my sense of compassion failed me. I dressed her in a hand-knit fisherman's sweater, two sizes too big, and an equally heavy pair of woolen pants, gumboots, a toque and the mandatory floater coat. Her petite frame doubled in size. It was a normal day for us: a trip across the choppy water and then a ride in our dilapidated pickup uptown. As we traipsed around Rupert, the day was warming up considerably. All of a sudden, my mom sat down on the curb and started to cry. "I can't do this anymore! I can't walk around dressed like this! I'm expiring!" she wailed. When I remembered this, I tried to apologize to her at her grave.

My love for clothes and everything aesthetic have always been a part of me, but, living in a rugged place, practicality trumps fashion. The Prince Rupert attire for commuting across the water was heavy duty raingear, boots, and often long woolly underwear for warmth. The only fashion statement we could make was wearing a hand-knit, handspun toque or sweater. No makeup, no nail polish, no fancy haircuts. Being natural and youthful helped in a place where the lighting was poor and the mirrors hard to find. I dressed from the local thrift shop, which I must have combed through weekly. I still cared enough to have a few outrageous outfits that gave me a thrill under my Helly Hansens when going to a party. We didn't pay too much attention to looking sexy. Since most of our clothes were loose fitting, most of the time breast size was not an issue as it is today. At least not for the women! Being so active left no time for looking in the mirror. There was a freedom in this. In Prince Rupert, I wasn't bound to the latest fashion trends or anxious about my appearance, or even compelled to brush my hair.

Prince Rupert provided many opportunities for us. We could make excellent wages. One of my first chances to be a feminist was working at the pulp mill as a labourer. There I was the only female amidst all the men loading 50-pound bags of salt. What a huge feat for me! That job was short-lived but I liked the paycheques and eventually spent most of my spring and summer working at the local canneries.

If my parents only knew how I looked! Dressing shloompy (comfortable) was necessary for doing our chores, but I have to confess that I hated the unstylish cannery uniform I was forced to wear. There was something so unattractive about the company overalls, rubber gloves, boots, and a bandana hiding my curly hair, and by the end of the day smelling that nauseating fishy perfume. It was not an easy job by anyone's standards, squeezing herring roe or cleaning salmon standing in one spot all day in a damp room with fish guts flying, slime, and sticky fish scales. All your limbs ached from the damp cold temperature. One season I convinced the floor lady to give me the task of picking up the trays, a job that required moving around. What a difference that made! Cannery work gave me financial independence and a chance to work alongside many ethnicities. I felt part of history working at Sunnyside Cannery, one of the last operating canneries on the Skeena River.

Between seasons, I was busy at Crippen Cove helping Bill build our house in the woods and becoming comfortable with a hammer, chainsaw, and other tools. I was finally learning how to be handy, developing muscles, skills, and a sense of achievement. Remember my childhood where

Shelley heads to work at the pulp mill.

my parents would call someone up to change a light bulb?

What a huge learning curve for all of us living without power. One of my first experiences with canning was cleaning and cutting up our neighbour's pig. He raised it from a piglet, feeding it spilled grain from the grain elevator in town. We made salted ham, bacon and headcheese from the bits and pieces of that poor little pet. There we were, two women, burning the midnight oil, reading how-to books, operating a tin canner, and following recipes that were completely foreign to me. It was a strange process of acculturation, preparing and eating pork.

Shelley becomes comfortable with a chainsaw.

I baked bread, canned and pickled fish, brewed beer and wine, preserved, dried and grew organic food. The hours in a day were busy looking after our everyday needs.

The decision to enter the teaching profession came after years of labouring. As a teacher, I worked for six months in Kitkatla, a village on a small island 50 miles south of Rupert. This was the aboriginal community where I learned about identity, respect, and the connection we all have with the land.

Eventually my middle-class roots re-asserted themselves and I wanted to be closer to my family and have a family of my own in a bigger city. Those 10 years living in Crippen Cove allowed me to find myself, and gave me experiences and friends I will always cherish.

Setting the Tone

by Janet Simpson

NO DECISION I HAVE MADE has had anywhere near the impact on my life as my decision to move to Prince Rupert. I swear I use no hyperbole at all. In terms of acquired skills and interests, relationships, and career directions, living in Rupert set the tone. Way led on to way. Here I am, on the eve of retirement, reflecting on the multi-faceted impact my adventures in the Town Without Pity had upon my life.

I don't think I had any sense of Prince Rupert or, indeed, the north coast, before marrying Mark in 1975 when we were both 20 years old at U.B.C. Mark had lived most of his life in Masset and Rupert and was able to find work at B.C. Packers in Port Edward every summer to earn money for university. I had worked in the Marine Building in Vancouver for a summer typing for the B.C. Forest Service, so in the summers of 1975 to 1977, I continued that work in Prince Rupert at their office on First Avenue East. During those summers, we lived with Mark's parents at the end of Graham Avenue. Working downtown provided me with the ample opportunities required to stuff the ballot box at The Bay on Second Avenue West, and I won their prize — a red 16-foot Grandmere Quebec canoe. As a Simpson, I also became a golfer (of sorts) and apparently started to inflate my own reputation as an athlete.

When we graduated with bachelor degrees from the secondary education program at U.B.C. in 1978, Mark easily landed a job at Booth Junior High School and I was offered a job at Prince Rupert Secondary School teaching English to the first Vietnamese people in town. I was a qualified

English teacher, but E.S.L. didn't really exist at the time, so I had to be creative, making lesson plans out of Pat Benatar's "Hit Me With Your Best Shot" and bringing in the gym teacher to give free haircuts. Mark and I moved into the apartment building behind Digby Tower, and I became good friends with Carol Manning, who was teaching home economics at Prince Rupert Secondary School.

During my first pottery class at the Civic Centre on a winter's day in 1978, I met a couple who were to become my life-long friends: Barb was a teacher's assistant at King Edward Elementary School, and Ron was a health inspector with the government, whose advice about which restaurants to eat at was always taken seriously. Many wonderful weekends were spent with their Lhasa Apso, Gartok, canoeing up the Exchamsiks and Khyex Rivers off the Skeena, and cross-country skiing at Hudson Bay Mountain in Smithers and along the Work Channel Road.

Mark and I split up the next winter, just after buying a pretty blue house at the top of the bluff on the east side of McBride Street. I moved in with Patti and Della, two kindergarten teachers. Over the next 18 months, the three of us single women lived in rental houses on Eighth Avenue East and then on Overlook Street, each dubbed Heartbreak Hotel. Somehow we managed to dance the nights away at Bogey's and T.J.'s without losing our jobs or our minds. Questionable relationships took shape and then exploded. We started to think of Rupert as a Town Without Pity. But life was especially fun when the young Quebecois came to town to work in the canneries and play in the coffeehouses. The Hallowe'en parties at Solly's were much anticipated, and there was often a good dance band at the Surf Club. Patti and Della decided it was time I learned to drive — alternating one day in Patti's automatic and the next in Della's standard. Some of Rupert's infamous hills were a bit hard on patient Della's clutch. Barb and Ron kept us all entertained: the curried lamb dinners and Jimmy Buffet/Leonard Cohen-laced evenings at their cozy home on Seventh Avenue East were legendary.

Carol also decided it was time I learned how to make salmonberry wine. The wine we made from the berries we picked along the railroad tracks and the prolific bushes in Skunk Hollow (under the Second Avenue bridge) made a product with an alcohol content I haven't since managed to duplicate. It packed an unbelievable punch; however, I'm still uncertain as to whether it was thanks to the super-plump salmonberries or some trackside herbicide.

Della's older brother, David, was working as an engineer in Beaufort, Sabah, on the Malaysian coast of the island of Borneo, and Della invited me along when she visited him in the summer of 1981. A chance conversation with Kathy Copps, who was a teacher at King Edward, resulted in the three of us heading over to Asia that June, Della planning to return to work in Rupert in September, and Kathy and I extending the trip for the year. Kathy and I had met at a drama production in Terrace: she a compelling new actress, and I a clueless director. As you can imagine, it was the trip of a lifetime. From mountaintop monasteries in Hong Kong to water buffalo-shaped houses in Sumatra, from jungle hikes up Mount Kinabalu with the Malaysian army to giant cockroaches in Sydney and the Stone Forest of China, we travelled, returning home only to head off immediately to Laval University to study French for the summer. When I returned to Rupert in September 1982, Della had moved to Courtenay, Patti to Richmond, and Kathy, Barb, and Ron to Ontario. At the deli in the mall on Second Avenue West, where many monumental decisions were made, I met Elaine, the drama teacher at Booth, and moved in with her on Cormorant Street in the new subdivision. Work had begun on Ridley Island and the quality of single life was unsurpassed: there must have been 11 men to every woman.

I returned to teaching E.S.L. at P.R.S.S., and started volunteering as a Board member of Maud Bevan House, the newly-opened transition house for women. With this work and my participation in the local teachers' association, I was slowly developing a political awareness, which has since become more pronounced. I am sure this time in Rupert set the stage for my current involvement in the B.C. Teachers' Federation, the Enbridge Northern Gateway hearings, the Rockland Neighbourhood

Association, and various environmental organizations. It was also tempting to head south for warmer options in the summer, so I studied intensive Mandarin at U.B.C. during the summers of 1982 and 1983. Not entirely fortuitous, as I had heard that the government was planning to introduce

Janet canoes across Rainbow Lake.

Mandarin Chinese to the school curriculum; this decision later enabled me to secure a teaching position in Victoria, a very difficult district to break into.

I had never considered doing a master's degree, but it gave me a perfect excuse to take Ron and Barb up on their invitation to live with them in downtown Toronto for a year. Despite the admonitions of both friends and acquaintances there, in September of 1985, I returned to Prince Rupert after completing my master's degree in computer applications at the Ontario Institute of Secondary Education at the University of Toronto. They remained skeptical, even though I was returning to a full-time continuing contract in a time of fiscal restraint. But most of all, they simply could not comprehend how I would choose the natural beauties and camaraderie of small-town life over the obvious pleasures of Toronto.

It came as a bit of a shock to hear that all my students had since graduated and that I was now an E.S.L. teacher at Pineridge Elementary School. I moved into one of the character-filled cottages on the bluff across from my old blue house on McBride Street with two budgies and six finches. One of my wildest adventures of that time occurred on Hallowe'en night in 1985. Linda, one of my colleagues, invited me to a party at the seaplane base hangar in Seal Cove, and I invited Carol Manning. Carol and I drove out to Seal Cove after enjoying a scotch with Bill at their cottage on Second Avenue. Naturally, it was just below zero and raining. I was wearing ballet slippers, tights and a sparkly sleeveless top under a long, thin, brightly-striped silk overcoat. My face was painted in purple and green geometric shapes, and on my head was a tall, pointed black hat. I imagined myself as some kind of wizard. We had just entered the party, put our bottle with the rest on a table, and checked out the scene. There were lots of people in peculiar costumes, including a group of engineers in orange overalls. And that is all I remember, apart from taking a sip from my first scotch at the party and instantly feeling drunker than I had ever been. I could barely walk. Somehow I made it to the door and outside for some air. I put my hat on the seat in my car, luckily aware enough that I couldn't drive. Then I headed home on foot, along the railway tracks in the pitch black rain, beside the ocean. Sometimes I ran, often I fell and forced myself to get up again because it was so cold. About five miles later, I eventually emerged onto McBride Street (I don't remember this part) and somehow into my bed. I was awakened by the phone ringing. Carol had seen me leave the party and, becoming suspicious, had followed me out, but I was gone. She had alerted everyone at the party, who had gone out to look for me. She had called the police, who had reached me at home. It was quite clear that my drink had been spiked, and I credit Carol to this day for saving me. Her actions likely prevented whoever doctored my drink from achieving his goal.

Oh, yes, and I have to thank Carol for knowing instinctively that Bill, the young teacher who had just arrived from New Aiyansh, 97 kilometres northwest of Terrace, to teach sciences and math at P.R.S.S., was perfect for me. Officially we didn't start going out together until we ended up on the same team at a curling bonspiel. It was the morning after Kathy and I had watched the northern lights from where she lived on Hays Cove Circle, resulting in my sleeping in and arriving late and in disarray at the curling rink. Neither of us had ever curled before. It was the weekend of dancing together at the bars on Third Avenue West, where I lost one of my opal earrings from the time Kathy and I spent in Australia. One of the few sports Bill had yet to try was cross-country skiing, so he was very impressed with my having represented Rupert at Williams Lake in the B.C. Winter Games. Of course, like my golfing prowess, my true talent in skiing became evident when I confessed that I had skied in last, along with the young volunteer who was collecting the flags. It was the start of a lifelong romance. We celebrated our 25th wedding anniversary in March 2012.

Now we live in Victoria, where we moved in July 1987. Bill started teaching at Central Junior High School and I got a job teaching the first Mandarin Chinese program at Mount Douglas Senior Secondary. After the 2012 school year ended, I retired after 35 years of teaching.

It was a tough decision to leave Prince Rupert. It was the friendliest place I had ever lived. My mother describes it as clinging to a mountain at the edge of the ocean. To me, it epitomizes the fundamental, verdant reality of small-town life on the north coast. It shaped my life.

It was Rupert

by Kathy Copps

I LOVE TELLING RUPERT STORIES, but my favourite has an almost deadly ending: "...and Jacques aimed the gun directly at me, pulled the trigger, fired a bullet through the window into the kitchen cupboard and shot my jar of Skippy peanut butter."

Telling that story is easy, but I've never tried writing about it before. I know it will be challenging. Before I write about that bullet, I'll have to provide some context: "I froze when I saw a boat pulling into Crippen Cove and recognized it was Jacques dropping the anchor and lowering a skiff into the water. With my binoculars I could see that his eyes were puffy, his face was all red and blotchy. It was obvious he was in rough shape, wrecked from days of continuous drinking. And he had a rifle tucked under his arm."

But you won't know who Jacques is, and now almost 40 years later I hardly recognize him myself. Was he actually planning to shoot me? If I plan to write about moving to Rupert to teach, how do I explain ending up in such a terrifying situation? Then again, how can I leave out such a crucial chapter?

Attempting to write my Rupert story and the shooting at Crippen Cove has required some reflection and even a bit of insight. I have always told the "Jacques shot my jar of peanut butter" as a humorous incident, but now almost 40 years later, it doesn't sound funny at all. And neither do the other near-disasters from Rupert days which for years I have been reciting as if they were Lucy Ricardo-like adventures: my house burnt down, my boat blew up, my boyfriend tried to hijack an Air Canada passenger jet. They are wild stories all right, but now as I think back, I wonder how I ended up in such dangerous situations, nevermind how I even survived. Nothing in my pre- or post-Rupert life had ever involved such danger. But the story began so idyllically.

As the B.C. Ferry pulled into the Prince Rupert harbour early that August morning in 1975, the sun was shining. The town, dotted with pink and pastel buildings, stretched along the foot of a dark mountain, between blue water and blue sky. To me it was beautiful, like a picturesque hillside village perched along the southern coast of Italy. I had left Thunder Bay, and after travelling up the majestic Inside Passage and getting my first glimpse of my new home, I was confident that I had made the right choice in accepting a position with a remote school district on the northwest coast. Although I loved my hometown, I had always assumed that one day I would abandon it for life in a big city — probably Toronto or Montreal. But to my surprise, on my first trip to Vancouver, I had fallen in love with the coast and immediately fired off applications to every school board from Tofino to the Charlottes. In just a few days, I would be responsible for a group of 27 Grade 3 students. A new life of independence and adventure awaited.

From the ferry, I headed on foot up McBride Street directly to the school board office where I was told accommodation was sparse and the best option would be a 30-by-10 foot trailer on the outskirts of town next to a slough and an out-of-business A&W — not at all what I had imagined for the first place on my own. But the place was furnished, cost only $160 a month, and was within walking distance of the school. Inside an hour of arriving in town, I moved in.

The first few days in the classroom were terrifying. I tried not to let on, but I was convinced that at any moment my students would realize I had no idea what I was doing. I spent every evening and most weekends thrashing around in the rain, back and forth between home and school, trying to devise lesson plans that might be relevant or at least challenging and fun. Those precious students were so trusting and seemed to have such faith in me, but keeping a classroom organized and channelling the energy of 27 eight and nine year-olds was a major challenge. Life in the trailer was not going smoothly either. After I had singed my eyelashes and eyebrows lighting the mysterious propane stove, I had given up heating the place and decided that wearing a hat, gloves and a few woolen sweaters was safer. Despite the obstacles, I loved everything about my new life: walking to school to the sound of early morning ravens' calls; the earthy scent from giant cedar forests mixed with fresh ocean air; mist covered mountains; eagles soaring overhead; and the ramshackle beauty of the northwest coast gardens. In the evening I listened to C.B.C. radio and pored over teacher guides hoping that eventually this teaching business would get easier. I was so grateful for my students' resilience and patience with me. Every morning I would be given little slips of paper decorated with coloured hearts and flowers, with messages like, "I love you Ms. Copps." That reassurance was enough to get me through one more exhausting day. Teachers have a special connection with their first class and when I look at my picture of Division I I Grade 3 Conrad Street Elementary 1975-76, I can still remember the names of each of my students.

Although I missed my family and friends, I couldn't believe that I was on my own and felt an overwhelming sense of freedom. At home my father was the editor of the local newspaper and throughout my high school and university days I had been uncomfortable with a real or imagined social scrutiny. Rupert was liberating. It was the perfect destination for a politically and socially aware generation who rejected many of the conventions of our families. Because of jobs in the fishing industry, the town was thriving and offered a unique convergence of quirky characters from all parts of the country and globe. Rupert opened a remarkable window of opportunity in a special time and place.

The ocean shaped the identity of the town, providing a pervasive connection to thousands of years of northwest coast native culture, which was still relevant to the daily lives of my students and the entire community. At the same time Rupert was like a frontier town, still a bit of the Wild West. When the herring fishermen were in town, Safeway ran out of food, the credit union ran out of cash, and the liquor store ran out of liquor.

Almost from my first day in Rupert, I felt such a strong connection to the surrounding coast, ocean and forests, and I knew I would have to buy a boat and get out on the water. I had never had any inclination to own anything — not a car, a washing machine, or even a toaster, so this sudden inclination to buy a boat was a mystery and an intimidating goal. Except for northern Ontario canoe trips, I had had no boating experience.

Later that fall I spotted an ad in the *Daily News* for a small $300 skiff with a 'C' licence for fishing halibut. I went down to the Fisherman's Co-op dock, met with the owner and handed over the money. Of course I had no idea what I was going to do with the boat, but it turned out to be a lucky buy. Shortly after that purchase, the Department of Fisheries changed regulations and the 'C' licence would no longer be available for purchase. There was going to be quite a return on my innocent investment.

One Sunday morning, friends who knew of my boating obsession invited me to go crab fishing at the mouth of the Skeena: my first ocean adventure. I went with Lorenzo, a local fisherman, and Jacques, his French Canadian deckhand. Jacques was tall and thin with thick dark braids to his waist. While he picked up the traps and sorted through undersized specimens, he held each one and spoke to it as if it were a treasure he was returning to the sea. He entertained us with a repertoire of Edith Piaf songs, and never stopped talking, laughing, drinking and smoking. My last boyfriend had been a teetotalling vegetarian; this guy was the total opposite, and I found him captivating. I did notice, however, that from one angle his face was symmetrical and handsome but from another, he had the profile of a smashed-up crow. He was an intriguing combination of opposites. In some ways he seemed so familiar, a link to French Canadian roots on my mother's side of the family, but I also sensed an alien recklessness and knew that I shouldn't go anywhere near him. Unfortunately, when he offered to help with my boat I couldn't resist, even when my friend who claimed to read auras said his was "black and full of holes."

When the school year was over, I had moved into a small house on Seal Cove Circle and stacked all my boxes of teaching materials inside on the porch. One night I awoke to what seemed to be the sound of rustling leaves. Within seconds I realized the noise had become an unearthly din and when I went to investigate I saw with horror that flames were shooting in the front door and the outer kitchen wall was enveloped in a roaring fire. Within seconds the blaze was devouring the old wood frame house and my only escape was through the living room window. I jumped and safely landed without a scratch on the sloping ground about 15 feet below. Looking up at the glowing inferno I had little doubt that one of Jacques' carelessly-tossed cigarettes was responsible.

In those days we didn't know about bad choices, but getting involved with Jacques was like being sucked into a vortex. Because I was so preoccupied with teaching and he was away fishing most of the time, I wasn't too concerned that the relationship was risky. Yet I didn't know anyone who started drinking in the morning. Then again, I didn't know anyone who was funnier, more generous or thoughtful, an accomplished chef, a poet, a voracious reader of French and English literature, and an extraordinary worker. Sometimes when I would go to visit my friend Maureen, while we talked in the kitchen he would wash and wax all her floors, sew missing buttons on her husband's shirts, or make a big pot of soup.

Jacques was so capable, yet he would constantly sabotage his own success. Too often he would pour his soul into a project, then suddenly let go and disappear into darkness, giving up just steps away from reaching his goal. It was heartbreaking to watch.

Despite his constant setbacks, I kept moving ahead with my boating obsession. With the sale of my 'C' licence, I had upgraded and bought a 30-foot rebuilt fishing boat. My hand was shaking as I signed the $4,000 cheque. It was a breathtaking expense, and although my plans for the boat were vague, I was still confident and single-minded in my pursuit of exploring the coast. Jacques' help was invaluable. We spent most of our time painting and repairing the *Dewey Mist*: it was in fine shape and, after the fire, offered an ideal, temporary living space down at the Cow Bay dock. In such confined quarters, I became aware of the vast amount of alcohol Jacques consumed. He was drinking all the time, but because he never

seemed to be drunk, I didn't think it could be too serious a problem. For days he would be in a great mood, totally focused and energetic. Then suddenly, without warning, he was paralyzed, silent and brooding. I chose to be blind to these warning signs and continued

Kathy explores Langara Island.

with plans for at least one major boat trip before school started. Just before we were to head out on an expedition to Langara Island, a beautiful halibut fishing boat, the *Francis W*, went up for sale. I fell in love with her, aware that a purchase meant heading in an entirely new direction: commercial halibut fishing. I wasn't at all keen, since halibut sometimes lived to be hundreds of years old, weighed up to 700 pounds, and when caught had to be clubbed or hog-tied. Eventually, I decided to buy the boat, hoping Jacques would stay focused enough to equip it and take it out on the remaining halibut openings that summer. In the meantime I thought some distance between us would decrease the pressure he seemed to be under. I moved to a small house across the harbour right at the entrance to Crippen Cove. There was no running water or electricity, just a wood stove, logs to beachcomb, wood to chop, rainwater to collect, and half a dozen truly remarkable neighbours. I marvelled at their pioneer skills building cabins, planting beautiful gardens, and welcoming me into the warmth of the small community.

Jacques had a few mildly successful trips, but after each expedition I noticed he referred to the *Francis W* as his boat and made it difficult for me to have any access to it. The situation was tense. My parents (who had no idea that I had been spending my time buying boats or jumping from a burning house) had been urging me all summer to go home for a visit. I decided that the time was right.

A few days into the visit, I had an urgent call from Jacques. While he had the boat in dry dock to clean the hull, a spark had ignited the gas engine. The boat had been blown to smithereens. In a way it was a relief, though I had to digest the loss of the boat. Insurance would cover the loss, and I could sever all ties with Jacques and his catastrophes.

Kathy at Crippen Cove.

But disaster struck again when Jacques attempted a surprise visit to Thunder Bay. Because the flight from Prince Rupert was late, he missed his connection and spent too much time in the Vancouver airport lounge before boarding the plane to Toronto. When one of the attendants spoke to him, he made his usual joke about being with René Lévesque's navy. Not too many years had passed since the F.L.Q. Crisis and his meant-to-be-humorous comment was taken as a terrorist threat. Upon landing in Toronto, the R.C.M.P. boarded the plane, arrested Jacques, and charged him with the attempted hijacking of a passenger jet. I watched with horror as the story unravelled on the C.B.C. national news that night. When the hijacker was identified as someone from Prince Rupert, my parents jokingly asked if I knew him. I didn't know where to begin.

The story didn't end there. There was still my return to Rupert that fall. My attempts to avoid Jacques enraged him and resulted in that almost deadly shootout in Crippen Cove, a shattered jar of peanut butter, a peace bond, and a court case.

So many years later, it is still difficult to understand how or why I was caught in such a succession of dramatic episodes. There was a convergence of inexplicable forces, and for those of us who experienced that time and place, we explained it by saying with a shrug, "It was Rupert." Nothing more needs to be said.

Born in France, Made in Canada

*by Ghislaine
de Saint Venant*

HE WAS GOING EAST, SO I WENT WEST; no real purpose except my good friend Cécile was going to Walla Walla, Washington to teach, so why not go for the ride? The year was 1975, and I had given myself a whole year off after receiving my degree at the Sorbonne. I had always wished to go to Alaska since I was a child; may as well go for that old dream as I did not have a fresh new one anymore.

I Greyhounded and hitchhiked my way through the States west and then east again, and back through the wild Canadian landscape. Thank you, Greyhound — $90 for a 90-day pass.

By the time I arrived in Banff, the bus pass ran out. I met a couple of German guys and we hung out for a few days. Soon after, I was ready for the Pacific and a ferry to Alaska. A nice truck driver picked me up in Smithers and dropped me right at the ferry terminal in Prince Rupert. I had somewhat boldly insisted on the drop-off spot, wanting to stay as short a time as possible in that northern neck of the woods that did not appeal to me at all.

How small coincidences in life always have a way to foul your plans.

I was furious to find out that the next departure was three days away! As I sat there wondering what to do next, a guy pushed the door.

"*Guten tag*, Ghislaine."

"*Alea jacta est*, Norbert." Yes, the German from Banff!

He assured me that I would be welcomed in Salt Lake, where he was hanging out amongst a few other "end of the road" like-minded people, squatting on that little tip of land across from Prince Rupert.

The next day I was asked: "Would you like to come along for a sail this afternoon?"

"Sure, I love sailing!" I hopped on board a little wooden sailboat named the *Mire Nime*, we left the dock, raised the sail, and the wind pushed us nicely. I was cold in my only shoes, so I borrowed a pair of socks from Modestus, who would become my close companion for the next three years. I sat on the gunwale but never had time to slip on the socks, I fell backward into the chuck. It was August but it felt much colder than the frigid winter Mediterranean waters I knew! Modestus yanked me back on board. What a good start! We did not come back at dusk as I expected, we kept going and going and going for three splendid months.

By then my life had been turned upside down and inside out, exactly what I needed to flush six years of boarding school and an ultraconservative French background. At last I was catching the 1968 wave of French revolutionary spirit, but in a northwest coast fashion. It was out of this world, completely irrational but here I was, embracing whatever came along with open arms.

We landed on Stephens Island, Skiakl, my home for two and a half years: the most intense, exhilarating, scary, difficult, crazy, foreign, liberating, revitalizing period ever. I had left my home, Paris, merely three months before.

Everything was original to me: walking barefoot in the thick, glowing moss; drinking cedar water right from the creek; eating wild foods I did not even know existed; digging luscious clams at low tides; tasting chewy chitons and ugly sea cucumbers; excitedly catching salmon or rockfish; drying what we could for the coming winter on strings, garland-like, above the barrel stove; handsawing firewood with an old but vital Swede saw; dealing with no-see-ums that were devouring me alive (the buggers love new warm foreign blood and only

The cabin at Skiakl.

rum could cure me of their nasty, sucking itchiness that was literally making me mad); learning how to cook on an old wood stove; splitting wood with an axe; washing my few ragged clothes in the creek, brown with cedar stain; discovering the pleasure of wood carving; helping make a harpoon out of whale bone to hunt sea lions. I was scared to go out at night as I was afraid to face the bright golden shiny eyes of wolves. I mumbled in my new language, English. Two people alone on an island trying to figure each other out: this was indeed my first try at that difficult and necessary life skill. I learned to accept my ignorance while reviving old, traditional skills: catching, skinning and curing mink and seal skins; deciphering the Foxfire series; canning wild geese killed with a bow and arrow, if not a crossbow; confronting enormous storms in that little sailboat with just a pair of 12-foot wooden oars; facing three massive humpback whales surrounding the tiny plywood skiff I found myself in. Everything was foreign, everything made perfect sense.

That was the point: no modern implements, gas engines, motors, or electrical gadgets that make life "easier." Going back to basics, really basics.

I am forever thankful that I went through this thorough cleansing early in my life. This period made me understand and appreciate the importance of simplicity and freedom. I also learned to be conscious of my surroundings, and developed an ecological awareness that has never left me.

We would come to Prince Rupert every few months depending on our supplies. On the rail tracks to the grain elevator in Rupert, we would collect free wheat berries from spills from the rail cars that we would ultimately grind in the hand-cranked stone flour mill to make delicious, heavy, free bread.

As many of us did, I got a job at the Port Simpson cannery pulling herring roe for the Japanese market, during that short period of intense raping of the sea. This was needed to buy the few basic staples. However, I was so disgusted by the whole business that I lasted a mere week. I sang old Gregorian chants as a meditation and for sanity, longing to go back to the peaceful, if not always serene Skiakl world.

We fixed and lived in a small log cabin built by Japanese men escaping the internment camps during the Second World War. Some very old

Japanese magazines, beautifully built stone walls, and a couple of cabins marked their lonely, sorrowful passage. The days were always filled with necessary chores but I felt enriched by a sense of freedom and ownership. Always I marvelled at the surrounding beauty of the place: the quiet fjord calm of sheltered waters, accessed by so few people; the thrilling beachcombing walks where the game was to find something purposeful or beautiful to take back to the cabin; the creative naming of some uncharted coves where we anchored such as "Bracelet Cove," where I lost my beautiful ancient silver bracelet from Madagascar, and "Glass Ball Bay," where all things Japanese would land ashore. We had a small transistor radio hooked to a six-volt battery which would last for a short while. Still, when I listen to the C.B.C. program "As It Happens," I remember trying to understand Judy Lamarche's high-pitched monologues.

Then I burnt out, my writing was getting crazier, my walking in the woods became stranger, this life was too intense for me, too rigorous, too lonely, the rawness was scratching my toughened skin. In retrospect, I had too many raw, different, wild, out-of-my-cultural-context issues to confront safely.

Not that I divorced myself completely from this rich and free lifestyle: progressively I just edged closer to town, back to Salt Lake, the squatting paradise across from Prince Rupert where the strongest friendships were created, where the best parties and community life evolved, and where we just went from one cabin to the other, whenever, to share the days, the chores, the skiffs, the meals, and the laughs.

Soon I was able to lie my way to some meaningless day-care work in town, a few days a month for an incredible paycheque of $90 that kept me going for a while. No jobs lasted very long then, life was easy enough: make sufficient money to keep going for a few months, then quit and look for another thrilling adventure. We were very fortunate to be so carefree, I wonder if it is still possible now? The whole idea was to make enough money in the shortest time possible for the longest slack time possible to reinvent oneself at our own 1960s speed.

Treeplanting was an answer, terribly hard work, but fun too once the little seedlings were heeled in the tough, destroyed earth, after the logging crews had done their ugly deeds. In this wilderness, freedom was a generic word: no taboos, but just the evident folly of living fully. The seasons were short for me, my body and my mind could not take too much of this back-breaking, rough and exhausting climbing up and down hills, tangled with depressingly dead conifers in a slaughter that seemed mindless, serving a so-called efficient and productive new world order.

This is where I met David though, soft-spoken, bearded, blonde with deep-set blue eyes, a spirited and idealistic man who became and still is my mate. Shortly after that first 1978 planting season, we set off in his trustworthy Falcon station wagon, exploring the wild hills of the B.C. interior before landing in Marcus, Washington. David was involved in a commune called the "American Village Institute," whose plan was to change the world. Weren't we all trying to change the world then?

The idea was to resurrect old ways and ideals: we took over an old high school, in a small, typical flag-waving American town, to live off our own hard work. We wanted to grow all our food, school our young, make tools and functional objects from wood and metal, and print on old presses the result of our new-found oldness. It surely became outrageous when we were melting, weekly, recovered metal scraps in a huge blast furnace to make cast iron parts for the lovely apple presses we were selling. What a blast indeed! We would pour iron melted at 1,000 degrees in sand casted molds, all this in shorts and sandals, it was too hot to be safety-conscious. Then China (rather, at that time, the Republic of Taiwan) copied our press models and we could not beat their price (sound familiar?), so we left. Nelson/South Slocan became home for a thrilling year while we took a furniture-making course. I still hear my father harassing me in one of his desperate letters: "So first you choose to live like the *sauvages* then you move up to melt iron and work with wood, might ever be a day when you will be back to the 20th century, perhaps?"

It was not long before the soft blue grey Pacific beckoned us back up to the northwest coast. Happy to go back to old, beautiful friendships, fun times and memorable potlucks and beach/cabin parties where delicious, healthy, fresh seafood of all kinds was so abundant thanks to all our splendid, crazy fisherman friends. We moved to Dodge Cove, dead serious to start a little woodworking shop. We made decisions easily then. We bought the old community hall (the Second World War army barracks that had been moved from Casey Cove to Dodge by the villagers), stuck on rotten pilings (42 of them!), and what a space: one half became our home, the other the shop. We bought a few machines (yes I was back to the 20th century) and made various wooden pieces to sell: turned bowls, stools, baby rattles, tables, chairs, cabinets. I especially loved the process of wood turning. I recall the incredible enthusiasm and energy both David and I felt contemplating our new creatively fulfilled life. We read voraciously anything about furniture making. However, the place needed a lot of painful labour to bring it back to some type of shape. This was hard work and sometimes difficult: extracting massive stumps from the muskeg with a stump puller (back to the 19th century) digging by hand six-foot deep holes, sinking in muddy muskeg (pre-Industrial Revolution?) to replace the rotten pilings. The mod cons were not yet up to date and we were made aware of that fact fairly quickly. When Amaury, our son, was born in November 1981, I stayed longer at the hospital as David needed to finish insulating. That winter was horribly cold. No running water so I would go to the little creek, break the ice and drop the chunks into buckets to be melted on the drumheater using wet, crappy, salt-laden beach wood in order to wash by hand the cloth diapers Amaury desperately needed (which century was that?).

Finally the place looked as beautiful as possible, a vast space for wild Hallowe'en dancing parties, a meeting place for our crazy and intense potlucks, or weekend-long Gestalt sessions where crying, shouting, laughing, reckoning, arguing were supposed to resolve all our personal and world problems. Intensity was the *mot d'ordre* but tight friendly bonds were never to be undone.

The thrill progressively faded and the hard work ate us up. We conceived a new awareness that other adventures could be fetched. For me, two dramatic events clarified the need to move on: in 1982 we had started, with a few friends, a small coastal tree planting co-op and this was quite fun and bizarre. I became forewoman, as I was still nursing Amaury, carrying him most days on my back. The forestry checker would show up, wide eyed and puzzled as to my sanity, mostly when he needed to hold Amaury tightly in his arms (stinking from lack of daily washing) while I was driving the pickup along rough logging roads (no baby car seats then). It all finished with a crash when my body seized up on my last treeplanting gig on Porcher Island. I was stuck in the bush by myself, the only way out a long downward crawl on my stomach. I was finally rescued by helicopter and taken to Prince Rupert where I lay for three painful weeks, drugged and miserable at the hospital. The other drama was the loss of our friend Brigitte, who ended her life in the woods behind our house. Much later, we fearfully found her scattered remains in the harsh wilderness that always seemed to be fighting back. We needed to leave, body and mind shattered, so we did in the spring of 1985.

Another adventure began in Vancouver, where we still worked hard, but in the late 20th century fashion.

Then Saltspring Island for the last 20 years where we decided to re-connect with our long ago survival/self-sufficient ideals, despite the fact that David commuted regularly to Vancouver while I taught at the high school. This summer our next folly/adventure is pulling us eastward, very much eastward, as we are moving to France from where all started for me, 37 long but essential and fortifying years ago.

Though I have not set one foot in Alaska after all, it's perfectly all right and I can only say with respect:

Thank you Canada, you made me who I am.

Ghislaine & son Amaury in a boat near Dodge Cove, 1982.

Mending Nets & Fixing Boats

by Linda Gibbs

IN FEBRUARY 1975, TWO FRIENDS and I set off up Vancouver Island in search of tree planting work. An old school friend, myself, and some crazy Irish guy I'd met working evening shift at the post office in Vancouver figured there was work up there. I had planted trees around Barkerville the season before this and thought that there must be some tree planting going on somewhere on the Island. We hitchhiked up the Island, stopping in small towns along the way, and even went all the way over to Gold River in search of work. It was too early in the season and as far as we could make out no one was even thinking about planting trees. So my school friend decided that Gold River was far enough and headed back to Vancouver. The Irish guy and I decided to hitchhike to the ferry that went to Prince Rupert from, in those days, Kelsey Bay. I had a friend who was working as a waitress in Prince Rupert and so I figured that we would at least have a place to stay once we got there.

I will always remember that first ferry ride to Prince Rupert. I had spent the last of my high school days in Vancouver and had been introduced to the Gulf Islands, so was familiar with west coast weather, but the mist hanging over the small islands, coves and inlets en route to Prince Rupert really intrigued me. I felt as though I was on my way to Japan.

Skipping ahead a couple of weeks or so after my arrival in Prince Rupert, with no tree planting work to be found in Prince Rupert or Terrace (another hitchhiking trip), I soon found myself immersed in the herring fishery. Up until then I had only just heard of herring, but I found myself jigging off the dock, down by Canfisco at the Rushbrook floats. I was on my way home on my bike with my herring catch, got the front wheel caught in the railway track, and my herring and I went for a spill. My herring dinner was now all covered with gravel. I picked myself up, dusted off the herring, and went home to eat my first and almost only fish catch during my 10-year stay in Prince Rupert. I soon found a job at Canfisco, squeezing the roe out of the little buggers — my introduction to the fishing industry. There we all were, dressed in white coveralls and red head scarves, which preceded hairnets (I have to say I prefer the head scarves). Working at Canfisco was also my introduction to unions. Then, I heard that there was work at the co-op, and they were paying 10 cents more an hour (a lot of money in those days). So I jumped the Canfisco ship and started a long-time relationship at the co-op.

I remember that I was sharing a house on Water Street above the railway tracks with a bunch of other cannery workers. I was working the graveyard shift, 8 p.m. til 8 a.m. Half of us at the house worked day shift and half night shift. As there were only enough beds for half of us at one time, things worked out pretty well. Some mornings after work, we would want to party so we had to wait until 11 a.m., when the Belmont or Empress Hotel bars opened, to go for a beer. We worked and partied hard and some cannery romances were sparked, but I'm not even gonna go there. The herring season went on and finally finished for me sometime in June. I left Prince Rupert with about $900 in my pocket and I felt like a millionaire. I went to visit my sister, who was living in Steveston at house called the Utopia Hotel. I felt so rich that I gave a her some of my hard-earned cash. It was about this time, with my pocket full of dough, that I bought a motorcycle, a 350 Yamaha Enduro. It had knobby tires and was not that great for riding on the highway, but later that summer I rode it, with the help of a friend, up to the Nass Valley, where some friends were building a log cabin. I spent the summer there and then ended up on Mayne Island in the Gulf Islands. The next spring I had my motorcycle shipped to Prince Rupert and went back to work at the cannery. I moved in to Grenville Court, which really was a funky old building. It was kind of across the road from the Savoy Hotel and next door to the Salvation Army hall. I think that Grenville Court had been either an old rooming house or maybe part of the Sally Ann's crash pad for destitutes. Second

Hand Al had some used and new junk that he sold in the bottom half of the building.

I rode my motorcycle to the cannery and back, but it was kicking the heck out of my leg when it wouldn't start. Prince Rupert's weather is really not the best for motorcycle riding so I sold my bike to another crazy guy, this one was from Israel I think. With the cash I got for it I bought my first boat, *La Lune*. I bought it from Sebastian, the local artistic guy, who

Linda sails La Lune *in the Prince Rupert harbour.*

had painted the name on upside down so that it read the right way up in the reflection in the water. So began my love of boats and the water.

It was a really lousy sailboat and it didn't row very well either, but it was how I first got to Salt Lakes. I was living with Larry then and, as he said , we would go out in the harbour "for a drift". Soon after my introduction to Salt Lakes, a place came up for sale. Places there were really squats. There had been a municipal park at Salt Lakes, before the road was built out of Prince Rupert. From what I understand there had been a ferry that would go over to Salt Lakes in the summer; some people had built summer cottages and there was a boardwalk that went up the creek to a lake. On big tides the water would go up into the lake, hence the name Salt Lakes. There is a little lagoon up there that I think was why the name was pluralized. Larry and I bought the little house at the top of the dock at Salt Lakes. The purchase included an aluminum speedboat with a 10-horse outboard and an unfinished house next door. The aluminum boat leaked like a sieve, and so we named it the *Sieve*. Now I was commuting across the harbour to work at the co-op: I was living my Dad's dream and my Mum's worst nightmare!

I worked the herring and salmon seasons and most winters went down to Mayne Island until the next fishing season started. Somehow or other the outboard engine was stolen from the *Sieve*, so I was boatless for a little while. But my friend John had found a really nice 14-foot rowboat in the yard by the sea cadets building and I was able to have it. It was a beautifully built carvel planked rowboat with two rowing stations, but it needed a lot of repairs. All of my good friends got together and helped as we put sister ribs in the skiff at Dodge Cove using a boat shed steam box to bend the ribs to fit. Bill was our boat guru and taught me so much about boats. We recaulked the skiff, puttied all the nail holes and put the greatest shade of green paint on it. Then I found some natural knees for the seats and put a coat of linseed oil on the inside and on the oars I had bought for it. We launched it and, boy oh boy, what a beauty she was. From then on I could be seen rowing all over the harbour, usually with my faithful dog Bubalina riding in the stern. One of my favourite rows was the trip to Crippen Cove taking the little passage called Gumboot Bay to get there. This little skiff I ended up calling *Stanley* and on two occasions won the rowing race during Seafest, once with Lorrie Thompson and once with Dolly Haraysm.

My partner Larry was a fisherman and fished for halibut and salmon, so he was away a lot of the time. I became familiar with outboard engines, chainsaws and living with no electricity. We had cold running water that we rigged up ourselves with a tote up the tiny creek that ran down the hill behind all the houses at Salt Lakes. I also became familiar with fishing gear and spent days with Larry when the boat was in town, overhauling halibut gear, sharpening and straightening hooks, splicing the ground line, and tying gangions to the longline. After a couple of years, Larry got his own boat and during some transaction or other in order to get a licence, I ended up with a 32-foot double-ended Fraser River gillnetter in exchange for some money that Larry owed me. The boat was called the *Naiad* and I *loved* this boat.

Shortly after it became mine, I put it up on the beach in front of Ken's house at Salt Lakes. It was a gentle sloping beach with few big rocks and as a novice I thought a great place to paint the bottom of the boat. I just drove it up on the beach and as the tide went out I jammed two-by-fours under the rub rail to keep it from falling over. As it happened all went well and I got the bottom painted. Later as I became more familiar with tidal grids, I was amazed that I had done the first painting on the beach. I used the *Naiad* to commute to town and Dodge Cove, and it soon became evident that the engine needed replacing. I don't remember where the new engine came from, but it was a Chrysler Crown and with much coaching from Bill, and the physical oomph of Bill and my friends, I installed the new engine. I hooked up the transmission and rewired all the electrics and was a proud novice mechanic when we turned the key and the engine boomed to life. It had a few small glitches. Every once in a while I would have to whack the starter with a hammer to get it to engage, but for the most part everything ran smoothly. I then built a new engine cover to a height that suited me, so that I could actually see out the front windows. I spent quite a bit of time on the *Naiad*. Wendy had taught me how to mend gillnets, and I soon found myself camped out on the co-op net floats mending nets for whoever would hire me. One summer, I would spend my day mending nets and then chug over to Casey Cove in the evening where Lorrie Thompson was caretaking the house and garden there. She had cabbage in her garden and crab pots in the cove and we dined royally on coleslaw, potatoes and crab. Mainly I used *Naiad* to commute around the harbour, but I did take the boat out to Stephens Island and took the infamous shallow pass to Skiakl a couple of times. Another time a group of us had a tree planting contract up Tuck Inlet and we used *Naiad* to get to the old logging camp where most of the others stayed, while I stayed on the boat.

As time went by I had more and more clients for my net mending business and a few of the guys heard about some net floats out at Port Ed that were free, so they towed one over to Salt Lakes. Salt Lakes soon was swamped by gillnetters, mostly friends of mine and Larry's. They would drop off one net and I would overhaul it while they fished the opening, then return to pick it up the next weekend. Sundays were hopping at our house. I would be up at the crack of dawn with the no-see-ums, mending away to get nets finished for the guys. Then when people started to stir, I would row back to the house in *Stanley* and make pancakes for everyone. The place was a hive of activity. When

Linda mends nets with the Naiad *in the background.*

everyone headed out for that week's opening, it was back to my lone self, net mending away on the float listening to C.B.C. to break the monotony.

During most of my years in Prince Rupert, I would head south for the winter as Larry had a place on Mayne Island in the Southern Gulf Islands. Later, I travelled to faraway places, to escape the winter rains. After some years I got to worry too much about the *Naiad* and having to have someone look after it for me while I was away. So I sold the *Naiad* to Thomas and Clara who lived out at Stephens Island. But I still needed a boat bigger than *Stanley* to get around the harbour and haul nets, so with some more help from my friends I ended up with an 18-foot Atkins-designed wooden skiff with a covered bow and stern that I named *Flo* after an aunt of mine; I named the outboard *Hardy* after my uncle. That skiff was a beaut and sadly the last boat I owned. It is of great consolation to me that the boat now belongs to Bill and Carol and still plies the harbour.

In 1984, I left Prince Rupert with a broken heart. I returned the next summer to work for a company that monitors tagged salmon returns.

I now work for the International Pacific Halibut Commission in Washington State. I go to the docks in Vancouver and Bellingham to meet returning halibut boats and collect their fishing logs, biological samples, and otoliths (earbones) from the halibut. I still feel connected to boats and the water. But I mostly work at a microscope where I count the growth rings of the otoliths to determine the age of the fish, all part of the data that go into setting fishing quotas for the following year.

My husband John and I host an annual Blackberry Festival, where old friends reconnect, along with their children and even some third-generation babies coming along. I will always cherish my time in Prince Rupert, Salt Lakes, Dodge and Crippen Coves for all the beautiful scenery and the incredible bonds I made and still enjoy with the people I met and loved there.

My Journey in the Northwest

by Francine Masse

MY JOURNEY TO THE NORTHWEST region of British Columbia began in February 1976. Two of my sisters who had come to Prince Rupert the previous year asked me to join them for their second adventure out west. Their idea was to work for a while in a fish cannery and then travel in Europe. However, I was not so sure if I wanted to leave my home and more specifically my family. I felt comfortable where I was. But, it was a time when young people travelled almost penniless hitchhiking across Canada, and for the mavericks that lived in Quebec, western Canada was new, was fresh. Without knowing it, I must have been one of them as my life in Prince Rupert was filled with adventures that I would certainly not have experienced if I had stayed in Quebec. And as long as the adventures and the learning kept happening, my travel in the west felt justified. However, despite the fact that my life in the northwest was attractive and stimulating, I still had some struggles. At times, I was torn between my family in the west and adventures on the one hand, and my birth family in east and culture on the other.

I still remember the day I set foot in Rupert. I felt like I was part of a movie scene. It was one of those winter days that make you want to stay on the north coast forever. You know, one of those days that only people who live in rainy places understand, a day that excuses all those rainy days that come by the month, a day that makes you hang around a little longer. The Coast Mountains with their snowy peaks were well defined against the deep blue sky; the air was clean and crisp; the water calm, letting the airport ferry sail smoothly; the north wind was present but not strong. I felt a sense of freedom.

During the first few months of living in Rupert, my sisters and I rubbed elbows with the French people who were also working in the canneries either during the day or at night almost seven days a week, trying to make in a month a salary equivalent to about three months of work in Quebec. During our free time we either explored the city or played pool at one of the many bars. After a month of living in a hotel, we met a west coast character that offered us to stay in his boat, the *Yankee Boy*, at New Float (Rusbrooke Float). His proposition was the start of many years of my sea life.

That is when and where I met my companion. To me, Steven was the epitome of the west: resourceful in the wild, contented when alone, at ease in the immensity of this country. He was the opposite of who I was: accustomed to city life, appreciating the company of others, and lost in the wilderness. Despite the fact that I did not fall in love with him right away, I liked his company, his qualities. He was fun, I felt comfortable with him. It was easy to talk even though my English skills were minimal.

In Steven's company, it was not long before I experienced some situations that were completely new to me, such as fishing halibut and salmon and living in the wilderness. The beauty of the surroundings and the sense of freedom and adventure led me to stay in the west. I was still traveling, I was still learning different things, and I was in love.

At the beginning, Steven and I lived like nomads. Depending on the seasons, we lived in different places: on the *Kanu*, our first fishing boat; at Osland on Smith Island, south of Rupert; and on the fish camp at Goose Bay on Dundas Island, a thing that now belongs to the past. Living at the fish camp was unforgettable. For six consecutive fishing seasons, for about four months at a time, with either a friend or family member, I lived away from civilization.

The fish camp was a barge with buildings on the deck: a small store with living quarters leading to a sundeck and a shed with pen boards that held a large supply of ice, as well as boxes to hold the fish. We weighed and bought fish from fishing boats that tied to the barge. We stocked and sold some fishing supplies and groceries in the store. We also sold fuel to the fishermen. Every day we baked apple pies that became locally famous, so much so that, once, a couple of fishermen quit their fishing early in order to buy some of them. Life on the camp was hard work, but interesting and rewarding and we got to know many fishermen, including some Tsimshian and Nisga'a people. I also appreciated the extraordinary side-trips during our breaks: exploring the north coast by skiff, motoring alongside dolphins, jigging for cod and halibut, trolling for salmon, picking abalone at very low tides, and swimming in a little secluded bay in saltwater warmed by the hot sand. I embraced this way of living without restraint. I had adventure, love, friendship, and a sister who shared this amazing time. I had more than I needed.

Sometimes adventure can become hazardous, as when the fish camp sank within minutes. We had a week of exceptional fishing: the ice shed and the boxes were all full of fish; even the aisles held fish as deep as our knees. Still the fishing boats kept coming. When the packer finally arrived, the skipper elected to quickly unload the new ice onto the barge behind the shed and take the fish aboard in the morning. With all the extra weight, the barge sank lower until the water began to seep in through the seams that were not usually submerged and consequently not watertight. We had a regular pumping regime, but didn't realize we were taking on more water than usual. We went to bed, and were awakened in the morning, on an angle, by the crashing of goods and gears falling off the shelves in the store. I went through the door that led to the roof and just had time to hand my infant daughter onto the packer we were tilting towards. My sister went down through the store and had to climb the high side to jump onto a friend's boat. Both boats barely had time to cut their lines. The barge sank and settled on the bottom, with part of the roof poking above the water. Unfortunately, we lost all our possessions, including several apple pies. Eventually, the barge was towed to shore and pumped out, and the abundant supply of pink salmon was sold. But for us, the season was over. We had a good scare but not enough to quit, as we did the job for another two years.

Having children changed my life. Steven and I had to look for a place to live, as the *Kanu* did not provide for our growing family. We decided to live in a deserted village, about three hours by boat from Prince Rupert, where friends of ours were caretakers. Living at Osland on Smith Island was challenging. I was a young mother with nobody to share this new experience with, other than Steven and our then-childless friends. And there were times when our only neighbours were the wolves who checked on us on their regular rounds.

Even though we were isolated from the big city of Prince Rupert, we sometimes had visitors. Osland brought also some social time. Those were good times. We would gather our friends and bring them by skiff to our place. We would spend the weekend eating and drinking, walking, making bonfires, and playing music. Then, it was time to bring them back to their world and me to return to seclusion and loneliness.

As time passed, I realized that I was missing the contact with others, especially young mothers who lived the same reality. Living in isolation was not what I wanted and I needed to get us out of there. I needed more to help me grow. Five years of living in Osland was enough.

We moved to Oona River, on Porcher Island. By that time, Steven and I had two children, Mandoline and Norah. Among other things, Oona River provided a community, including a school for Mandoline. Even at three hours away by boat from Prince Rupert, Oona River became the gateway to what I am doing today: my teaching job, my quilting hobby, and my desire to be an active member of my community.

Until living in Oona River, my friends were still the transient French people who came to work in the canneries and who stayed for a few years and then left. I was devastated when these friends left, as they were helping me keep my French identity. Living in Oona River gave me the opportunity to break away from that pattern. I started to realize that it was better to find friends who were similar in thinking and way of life than using only language as criteria. Consequently, my English improved. I became more self-confident and was ready to get involved in the community, such as becoming part of the Oona River quilting group, working on the salmon enhancement project, and teaching French to the English kids in Oona River.

Sadly though, Oona River was still not enough for me. My two children could barely speak French after living there less than of two years. I was starting to search for words myself. My culture is central to my growth, to my emotional state, and to who I am. It was important to me that Mandoline and Norah spoke French in order for them to understand all of my idiosyncrasies and it was important for me to maintain my language in order to nurture my identity. It was time to move.

Oona River prepared me for living in Dodge Cove, a small community 15 minutes by boat from Prince Rupert, where we lived for 17 years. It taught me the sense of community that I needed to live in a small place, in a place where each person is important to the whole. Dodge Cove was the place where we raised our children in a peaceful and secure manner among other families who came to live there with a similar intention.

Francine in Dodge Cove.

My life in Dodge Cove was full and ambitious. There was no time to feel isolated and culturally deprived. For the first few years, we had the seasonal routine of children and school in the fall, winter and spring, and fishing for one month during the summer with Steven. I have some wonderful memories of our family on our fishing boat, the *Bokay*, on the northwest coast of Haida Gwaii. The early rise to catch salmon, exploring beaches during slow fishing time, sailing among killer whales, storms that made my legs tremble uncontrollably, and playing the same games over and over again with the kids to fill boredom: all these moments were unforgettable. These fishing trips nourished my desire for adventures. Sometimes, Steven went fishing without us. That gave me the opportunity to be closer to the other women who lived in the same situation as I did. We shared suppers, we babysat each other's kids, we opened up to each other.

The big change that happened during those years is that I became more sedentary due to the children. With a more settled way of life, one has more time to know the people around. The women of the north coast had a tremendous influence on me. They taught me to be strong, to face my challenges and to expand. Our quilting group was very important to me. Not only were we creating quilts for good causes, but we were also sharing ideas, discussing and sometimes solving problems while drinking a glass of good wine and having fun. Moreover, these women helped ease the longing I felt for my faraway sisters.

It was also the perfect time and place for me to pursue my education. Moreover, I had found my passion in life: teaching. So for part of my life in Dodge Cove, I studied to become a teacher. Also, I was given the opportunity to volunteer at the French immersion program in town where my children were attending school. I had to persevere and overcome many obstacles to study in English, find a balance between family, work and university, and still try to fit in a social life.

I like to reminisce about the community work bees that were often organized on Father's Day. The schoolhouse, as we named our community centre, was the common ground for everyone in the Cove. It needed some care. So, out came the nails and hammers, the paint and paintbrushes, the lawn mower, and the hands to to rebuild, to paint, to prettify. These work bees were fun social events.

The schoolhouse also provided the place for activities and events, such as quilting, yoga, and our famous New Year's Eve community dance. With not much preparation and a good selection of music, we danced until our legs could make us move no more. I cherish the memory of those dances and miss them immensely.

There were certainly some moments of doubt, but for the most part, I was finally content and I thought Dodge Cove would be my home forever. But it is hard to anticipate the future. Mandoline and Norah moved away to the big city of Vancouver. Steven was re-evaluating his life as a fisherman. When I was offered a teaching job for the French school district in Kelowna, I thought it was time to catch the wave of opportunity that was presented to me. It was exciting to experience something new.

Was I happy to move somewhere else? Professionally and culturally, yes! But socially, I will never encounter another place like Dodge Cove. When I first moved away from Dodge Cove, and for the next two or three years after, I was mourning the north: the way of life, my friends, and even things that bothered me towards the end of living there: going across the harbour in the open skiff in the rain, pushing the wheelbarrow full of groceries, walking the same path every day. The north was for me like a very good book that I had just finished. I was not yet ready to start a new book because I still wanted to live the story and its characters a while longer. The northwest coast was the best story that happened to me.

The Last Resort

by Anneke Van Vliet

I WAS FEARLESS, CRAZY REALLY, young, in my twenties, city bred and I wondered sometimes how I had arrived from the sophisticated city of Montreal to this remote northern community thousands of miles away. I was a privileged baby boomer: educated, adventurous in a time of un-limited work and opportunity, yet it was one of the most emotionally and physically challenging times in my life. Challenging because it was the seventies and we were trying to do it differently, committed to a big social experiment in a hopeful time of unlimited possibilities. We were questioning everything — materialism, consumerism, war, religion, mar-riage, gender politics, sexual mores, political systems — it was all open to change. I found a group of fellow adventurers in Prince Rupert; we found each other.

It was 1976 and I escaped to Prince Rupert to get over a difficult romance. I was heading for the Queen Charlotte Islands but fell in love with Prince Rupert on the way. When I first arrived, I met the Salt Lakes community through a chance encounter with John — a devastatingly hand-some blue-eyed man who told me he was attracted to me and rowed me to Salt Lakes to initiate me into the community.

I embraced the community and eventually moved into the "Last Re-sort," a one-room cabin with an ocean view and everything I needed. We heated our homes with the floating logs of the high tide, towing them in and cutting them up together for our winter heat. I loved community wood days — topless (hey the men could do it) chopping, carrying, stacking in organized chaos. To this day I can split any piece of wood, no matter how knotted or challenging, a skill from my Prince Rupert days. I loved the smell of the wood, particularly the sweet cedar that tinkled as it split apart. I loved the camaraderie, the laughter, the feeling of being strong, powerful, independent and self-sufficient, and I loved the connection with this group of people, mostly from cities across North America, who had migrated to this remote northern community to live off the land and embody the hippie dream.

Boats provided our transportation and I quickly learned to read the water and the weather. Fog terrified me. I had fearlessly weathered many storms arriving at work soaked and caked in ice and motored home without a light in pitch black, managing to avoid the deadheads, but fog was the worst. I remember crossing the water early one morning in the fog. I was in my boat, *Magnolia*, a sleek 14-foot wooden skiff, heading across the harbour in the fog to work at the post office. I had to get to work — the Protestant work ethic of my industrious Dutch immigrant parents is entrenched in my psyche. I was trapped in a misty white shroud that left me feeling disembodied, disoriented, and at the mercy of passing boats and, worse, freighters. I hoped a freighter would recognize my boat on radar but thought it more likely that I would register as a harmless floating log. I did a complete circle three times with the treacherous Salt Lakes rocks looming up unexpectedly each time though I was sure I was heading in a straight line for town. By the third time, I finally gave up and headed home to my cozy cabin. At noon the harbour police showed up to make sure I was still alive. Worried, my colleagues at the post office had sent

Anneke's kitchen in her Salt Lakes cabin.

them. No cell phones or landlines, no computers, no electricity: no way to report that I was all right.

Fishing and the spillover industry were the life and heart of Prince Rupert; everybody fished or worked the canneries. My first spring, I worked the midnight shift at the co-op cannery for herring season – it was good money with lots of overtime. My friend Stu hosted an all-night C.B.C. radio show and he would dedicate songs to us as we worked on the cannery line picking herring off the conveyor belt to squeeze out the roe. It was damp, cold, noisy work. We had moved into town to Grenville Court, a large communal house off the main street. The house stank of fish (we called it the smell of money) and

Enjoying an outdoor bath in Salt Lakes.

the hallway was piled with stacks of gumboots, aprons, overalls, rubber pants, jackets and gloves. I shared a bed with Bill and Shelly; when they rolled out in the morning, I rolled in.

Rolling in and out of relationships was common in Prince Rupert. Marriages came and went. At that time, adultery was the only grounds for divorce. To help my friend Greg, I went to court willing to describe in detail our non-existent adulterous affair. We had planned a story of wild sex on the kitchen table, but unfortunately they never asked for the details.

I did eventually visit the Queen Charlottes by hitching a ride on a small oil tanker. These were pre-ferry days and seaplanes were expensive, so my friend Carol and I wandered the docks and found a free ride. Best accommodations we ever had: our own room, home cooked meals and a ship full of men dedicated to our safety and comfort.

I lived in Prince Rupert for three years, only three years, but it had and still has a huge impact on my life. The experience solidified my values and my political views: I still believe in world peace, social justice, sustaining our environment, and the value of community and simplicity. The most profound legacy of my time in Prince Rupert is the tribe of friends that still surrounds me 35 years later. It is a community with the normal dysfunctions – hurts, angers, misunderstandings – but grounded in acceptance and trust, the product of 35 years of intimacy. Outsiders comment on the uniqueness of my community and I take it for granted; it is part of me and my life. But most of the time I am just very grateful.

From Skiakl to Dodge

by Wendy Brooks

WHAT DREW ME NORTH was adventure, the desire to go somewhere new and different. I don't like big cities and I felt the need for wilderness and lots of space with few people.

As a child, my family moved from Victoria to Ottawa to Winnipeg, and back to Victoria. My father worked for the federal government as a national parks planner, so my family often spent the summers travelling across the country, going to various national parks, camping and hiking, before it became so popular and crowded. I didn't think so at the time, but I guess I got used to the feeling of being outdoors a lot, in natural surroundings. Later on, I worked as a park naturalist while I was going to post secondary school.

My big leap from urban to rural life came when I was 23; I moved to Rock Creek on the Kettle River. I left an indoor art school to paint outdoor landscapes, and to experience cabin life. Several groups of like-minded people set up cabins or bought land in the hills around the valley. Like many people in Canada and the U.S. at that time, especially ex-suburbanites, they tried to live simply, off the land. It felt right to me. I learned to gather and store wild foods, some basic vegetable gardening, how to place bulk food orders with friends, and how to put chains on my Volkswagen van to drive in the snow. We got used to living without electricity and running water in all four seasons. Some of us even swam naked in the river, partied wildly at the Rock Creek Hotel, danced on the pool table, or skinned a rattlesnake on the front steps. Relationships formed and split; like the ice on the river, each spring there was a new spring breakup. I didn't do much painting.

Eventually I moved on, thinking I should revise my life skills and educational goals. I moved to Kelowna for a winter to pick up some science courses to puruse animal sciences work, as a veterinary assistant. I got my courses, but lost interest in institutional learning. I worked part-time at a greenhouse, a horse stable, and an orchard: all these jobs paid poorly.

Then, while playing pool, I was attracted to one of the many young Quebecers that came to pick fruit every year. It was a circuit many undertook, from Quebec to B.C. and back again, often with a stop in southern Ontario to pick tobacco. In the spring they went to Prince Rupert to work in the canneries, or crew on fishing boats. The hours were long, the pay was good and the parties ran into the wee hours. When Yvon said he was headed that way, I was ready to go. Rupert was a rockin' town in those days, people came from all over, and the fishing industry fuelled the town. For accommodation, the extended French connection led us to a back road by Prudhomme Lake where there were cabins to rent, mostly by the Quebecers. We found an abandoned school bus at the end of a trail and made it livable by stretching plastic over the empty windows and installing an airtight stove. It was at this time that I found a strange piece of jewellery lying on a pathway, a heavy brooch set with a large blue stone.

Most of us found work at the fish canneries in the Rupert area. I worked at the Nelson Bros. B.C. Packers plant in Port Edward. There were long shifts, often standing 12 hours in gumboots and company jumpsuits, handling fish beside other women of all ages. I remember the slightly metallic smell of fish mixed with the scent of the cardamom seeds that the East Indian women chewed. And the taste of very bad cannery coffee. Over two

Wendy at Prudhomme Lake.

seasons at the cannery, I met a wide range of people: fishermen and women, sailors, travellers from all over the world. In 1978, I also worked with an environmental group bent on stopping oil tankers, called S.O.S. (Save Our Shores). I also tried lobbying the City to start a recycling program — but it wasn't interested. Then I met another unusual character living on the fringes of this northern community.

At the end of my second year of the fruit picking and cannery work cycle, I went to a party one full moon night at a house rented by some twins from Montreal. Towards the end of the evening, as I was leaving and about to climb into my old blue 1967 Chevy station wagon, I met Des. We stood in the rain and talked about weather, windshield wipers, and the full moon in July passing through the constellation of Capricorn — he was a Capricorn. His curly blond hair, bare feet, gumboots and life on a sailboat intrigued me. Then, I met him again at a party at Salt Lakes.

So I didn't go to Quebec that winter as I'd planned. I returned, alone, to Prince Rupert after the fruit picking season, with cases of canned fruit and tomatoes, a few of my worldly belongings, and my dog Rufus. I was 26. In early November 1978, I chartered a small float plane to fly to Stephens Island, about 30 kilometres west of Prince Rupert, where Des lived in a rustic log cabin.

Except for going to work in the fishing season, Des stayed on the island year-round where he made silver jewellery. He had been alone at his cabin for a least a month, so when I landed in the small narrow bay with the supplies I'd brought for a visit of a few weeks, one of the first things he asked me, after a warm greeting, was, did I bring any tobacco? Mutual friends had already given me the heads up so, yes, I had.

On Stephens Island, part of Skiakl Bay has a long narrow pass, where the tides rush in and out twice a day. The land is treed but windswept, as it faces the wild Hecate Strait. Little rocky bays and sandy beaches or long grassy intertidal flats abound. Quiet, but for the raven's barking call, it was the wilderness I longed for — I was totally enthralled.

His dog Sambo and my dog Rufus were instant friends. The cabin was cozy, one room, built simply with logs and cedar shakes, likely by a mink trapper in the forties. Des and his former partner Ghislaine had "modernized" it with wall hangings, cushions, low furniture, and a loft. Life was simple. Survival was dependent on daily routines of hauling water, hand-sawing beach logs with a huge two-person saw, chopping wood, fishing for food, and tending a garden. Nights were tranquil with candle and kerosene light, a wood stove, and many hours of listening to C.B.C. radio. One day I showed Des the brooch I had found on the trail at Prudhomme Lake. It was his — one of the first he had made, and the beautiful blue stone was lapis lazuli.

Wendy & Des outside their cabin at Skiakl Bay.

By spring of the next year, for the first time in many years, I did not feel the pull of spring fever or the need to move. Des capably sailed the *Mere Nime*, a 26-foot sailboat counting the bowsprit, with a Marconi cutter rig, without a motor but with 11-foot oars (sweeps). We had made several hair-raising sailing trips into Rupert that winter, where Des sold his Celtic style silver jewellery and we bought basic supplies to take back out to the island. Each time we arrived in Rupert I felt culture shock. It seemed that city living often meant turning off from one's surroundings, to the overload of noise, smells and lights that cities have in abundance. Even walking on pavement felt odd. On the island, our senses were acutely tuned to the whole environment, especially sound, to inform us of changes in the weather or of the nearness of wolves, ravens, geese, sandhill cranes, or people.

Over the years, we did have neighbours who lived across the narrow bay and around a turn of small islands. Thomas, Clara and children Blake and Rachel came and went over the years, and lived a similar existence to ours. Elf and Maggie arrived after a long trip up the coast from Vancouver in a small wooden boat, towing a row boat of belongings. They set up in another tiny abandoned cabin at the foot of a waterfall. Karl and Sheila moved out a few years later and built a lovely cabin in a tidal bay which emptied when the tide went out to give up a large sandy flat covered in periwinkles. Skid and Dory felt the pull to give island life a try and took over Thomas and Clara's cabin when they left. Steve and Laura started a cabin which Steve lived in by himself for a few years. We met for dinners around campfires or for trips to sandy beaches together, but often went days without seeing anyone. We were all very in tune with the land, the seasons, the weather, the wind, the animals, and various means of gathering and storing food. But the ocean, its currents, its beauty and its power, was what really determined so much of our existence.

When I became pregnant, I was very healthy in body and mind, but recognized that my part in our physically demanding lifestyle was going to change. Because I had a previous miscarriage, we decided to move closer to a hospital for the birth. We had friends living in Dodge Cove on Digby Island and we were able to house-sit for the month before the baby was born. The night of the birth, I was knitting, then put it aside and stood up. My waters broke and my labour began. I felt euphoric, my vision both crystal clear and in a bit of a blur as Des scurried around gathering things for the trip across the harbour to Prince Rupert. It was about 9 p.m., a dark and quiet spring night. It was difficult to walk with the frequent contractions, so I settled comfortably into the wheelbarrow and Des took us off at a trot. By that time, we had a small outboard motor, a British Seagull, installed on the sailboat. The crossing was comfortable, gently riding up and down the swells of the harbour, an image I would return to during the contractions of labour. As Des tied up the boat, I remember thinking it might be nice to just stay and deliver in the boat, but we didn't. It was April 9, 1981 and, as it turned out, it snowed during the night. We almost named her April Snow.

Bronwyn was born at 1:27 a.m. on April 10 attended by Des, his sister Jolanda and Dr. McLean who was supportive of our natural birth. Our beautiful baby girl looked at us with eyes that define the phrase "deep pools of light." We were awestruck.

A few weeks later, as we pulled out of the harbour, sailing on our way home to the cabin on the island, I was overwhelmed with the sense of love and concern for protecting this new little being who depended on me so completely. I was 28.

For the next three years on Stephens Island we were a small family in a small community, happy and satisfied for the most part. Bronwyn grew and learned the same things we had living close to our environment. She was the first grandchild, so was the recipient of much love and attention from our families. Meanwhile, our neighbours had children and even raised chickens, ducks, goats and pigs — we stuck to chickens. For various reasons, some couples moved away until there were just two families left. One day, while looking at children in a Sears catalogue, Bronwyn asked, "Mom, where are the other kids?" She meant in the rest of the world, and I was struck by her longing.

When I became pregnant again in 1984, we planned on another town stay for the birth and to return home afterwards. We loaded our sailboat, took our two dogs and a cat, and towed our rowing skiff laden with two homemade crates of chickens. Fortunately, we had fair winds. We stayed at another house in Dodge Cove while Des worked at salmon fishing. Bronwyn had turned four and thoroughly enjoyed being with more children.

At an appointment with our doctor, he said, "There are too many arms and legs." The hospital didn't have an ultrasound machine yet, so I was a bit in denial that "it" could be two. But it was. My due date was in August. On July 10, Des was on his way home from fishing. Near midnight I was sewing a gift for my sister's wedding on the 13th when my mild contractions turned into major ones. I called upstairs to ask visiting friends to care for Bronwyn and help me get to the hospital. Phone calls in the night rounded up neighbours willing to give me a ride in a skiff to get aboard a fishing boat to get across the harbour. We also located Des sleeping aboard the boat he worked on, and called a cab for the ride to the hospital. The cab driver was quite freaked when Des told him I would "just finish this contraction" before I could get into the cab. The twins were born at 8:29 and 8:36 a.m., amidst a flurry of doctors and nurses who wanted to witness the natural birth of twins. Des held Rheannon and I held Thora. We were in love once again. The next day I called my sister Nancy in Victoria to say we definitely would not be able to make it to the wedding. I was 33.

We stayed in Dodge Cove while Des fished that summer and I looked after the girls. With electricity and running water, it was easy to keep up with the diapers and laundry that two babies can generate and Bronwyn was a helpful big sister. On the island, I had done all the washing by hand, including diapers, using a scrub board. But it became clear that returning to the island, as we had done with Bronwyn as a baby, meant considering major changes. To run a washing machine would mean operating a gas generator which we both felt was an intrusion on the wilderness life. We already owned a chainsaw and that had been an adjustment. So we decided to stay where we were for the winter. We went back out to our cabin at Skiakl Bay the next summer for the twins' first birthday. It was a lovely visit, but the decision had been made to live away for a while longer. We continued to visit often, but sadly, especially for Des, we never did move back.

Dodge Cove in the eighties and nineties was a great place for children, and other young families like ourselves, often with a fishing background, moved in. Our house was old and needed constant repairs, but we bought it anyway and raised our children in an environment with plenty of roaming space and neighbourly caring. With an unpaved road and very few vehicles, the main wheeled traffic was wheelbarrows and bicycles.

Des continued fishing and made silver jewellery in the winter. I was more or less content with community life, the birthday parties, making quilts, raising children, chickens and ducks, and tending a garden. For a while, it still seemed odd to mow a lawn instead of cutting it for hay and shopping at a grocery store rather than making my own food. By the time Bronwyn was school age, she clearly enjoyed the company of other children and so began the real introduction back into the system of modern life.

I sometimes say that I followed my children into the school system because I gave volunteer time before I began to work there. Before all three of our girls were in school, I was doing teacher-on-call work as an uncertified teacher, so great was the need for substitute teachers in the district. With the courses I took, and the encouragement I got from the teachers and other students, I decided to continue training as a teacher, which meant crossing the harbour at night in winter, from Dodge Cove to Prince Rupert, a distance of about 2 kilometres. There were some thrilling trips, sometimes with Kristin, Sheila or Francine, who were also taking night courses. Eventually I had enough credits and, with transcripts from my former university courses, I applied for the Professional Development Program at Simon Fraser University. In 1993, I finished it and in 1994 became a certified teacher, something I thought I would never do. I was 42.

In the meantime, Des bought his own salmon gillnet fishing boat, the *Vonni-Dee,* and was still fishing halibut on other boats as well. Part-time teaching worked for me, with our girls' lives full of school, dance, soccer and friends. Our life was predictable and consistent for the school years, and the girls all got the chance to go fishing with their Dad before he sold his salmon fishing licence in the government buy-back program.

Des now works in environmental politics. I've had over 15 years of continuous teaching. Each of our girls has moved away, has a career, more or less related to their university degrees, and are happily partnered. Des and I moved down the road to a beautiful waterfront house. I still keep chickens. In June of this year, 2012, I turned 60.

This is how I like to start my day:

If I get up before sunrise, I greet my morning cat, and we sit on the couch and have coffee while we consider our day ahead. As the sun rises over the mountains, a pair of ravens will arrive to scan the side deck for possible food scraps. Sparrows will flit across the picnic table for crumbs, and herons may cruise slowly over the house on their way to the beach. The pair of ravens sits on the woodshed roof together. One runs its beak up the neck of the other, its eyes closed. They pause, one ruffles the feathers of the other and with heads close, they seem in a state of bliss as one gives and the other receives. These things give me great peace and a sense of the world as it has been and will be long after I am gone.

Waterlogged Milestones

by Sue Staehli

I MOVED TO CANADA and got married when I was 20 because the border guards would only issue me a three day visa; but I wanted to visit my boyfriend indefinitely. When I called my mother from a phone booth later that day, she told me that my father would have liked to have been asked for my hand. Now that I am older than they were at the time, I know they were really just starting to realize how meaning slips away without rituals to recognize the milestones of our short lives.

When we arrived in Prince Rupert in 1977, we were on our way to the Queen Charlotte Islands after a summer of tree planting in the interior and a couple of winters squatting in abandoned cabins outside of Kelowna and McBride. The quintessential British Columbian work experience of the seventies, tree planting in those days was an unregulated free-for-all. We earned enough money for a subsistence lifestyle through the winter by hard physical labour during the summer planting season. We lived out of camping gear we had accumulated from former backpacking treks, cooked over campfires, bathed in whatever ice cold river or lake we could find while tormented by bugs and always on the lookout for bears. I had been a bookish young person, but along with academics I had developed a taste for cycling, skiing and hiking. One of the years that I attended college in New Hampshire I lived in a tipi instead of a dorm; my naturalist studies were a nice segue into living in the B.C. wilderness, learning how to live off the land as well as love it.

Our plans to spend the winter on Haida Gwaii were foiled by the difficulty and cost of getting the camperized Chevy half-ton truck we were living in across Hecate Strait. In retrospect, I wonder why we were so attached to its blue plywood bulk, but I suppose it represented all the comforts of home. I was six months pregnant and feeling like quite the odd duck, looking for a nest.

We drifted into work canning salmon at Cassiar Cannery, south of Port Edward, and then found a place to settle in for the winter in Dodge Cove. We made no secret of our intention to deliver our child at home in the primitive shack. When our friend Rick remarked that he knew the child had not yet been born because he didn't hear any crying, we responded smugly, "Our baby won't have any reason to cry."

Raven was born just as we had planned, introducing me to the knife-edge of experience that is a healthy labour. On one side of the steep ridge lies what could be described as pain, but on the other is a kind of psychedelic ecstasy. I could choose to look either way for my perspective on reality. There have been countless times in my life since then when I have drawn on the strength of that knowledge. At the same time, a shadow entered my life, because during trips to scope out prospective tree planting contracts, my husband began the first of a series of extramarital affairs and I did not have the self-confidence to assert my right to be a full partner in determining the nature of our relationship. My tearful objections were met with philosophical arguments that interested me enough to distract me from the fading of a dream of real intimacy I had perhaps taken too much for granted.

Even though, as a youth, I had identified in myself a tendency to take the easy road – when rock climbing I would avoid the shimmy up a chimney when there was a simple scramble up rocks with easy holds right next to it – in my late twenties my life became infused with struggle and effort. When Malcolm decided the Dodge Cove shack we were in was not suitable for long-term accommodations for a family and arranged for us to become the caretakers of an old coast guard installation neighbouring Casey Cove, I persisted in doing my grocery shopping using the water taxi from Dodge Cove, lugging a string-tied box at the end of each arm, with Raven strapped to my body in a Snugli. When the tide was full-in, the trip around the beach at Casey Cove was impassible and I took a trail up in the woods that linked to a power line cut to get us home.

By mid-pregnancy with my second child, we became the caretakers of the C.B.C. transmitter station up on the hill at the edge of the village. Suddenly we had electricity, hot and cold running water, flush toilets, and an amazing view in all directions. But when Alison was 18 months old I took a job across the harbour, which meant a complicated schedule of taking the children to various babysitters on the island by foot and rowing skiff. I then hitched a ride across the harbour and a ride into town, reversing that process every evening. In the summer I often just rowed across the harbour and then rode my bicycle straight to work and, without the waiting, it did not take so very much longer. I must have been very desperate to have taken all that on. I remember how terribly hungry I was every evening walking back up the hill, carrying my daughter and trying to get my three year-old to walk a little faster. Still nursing my daughter, I must have required a lot of fuel to keep up all that activity!

By 1982 we had become enamoured with fishing and purchased the 36-foot motor vessel *Havkat*, with a crab licence, and a five acre piece of property in Oona River. Soon after, we had moved from our comfortable hilltop residence and were living on a remote island four hours over water from town, dependent for transportation and income on an unfamiliar boat with an exposed diesel engine in the middle of the only quarters below-deck — and neither of us had ever caught a crab in our lives! We were dabblers in the arts of resource extraction that our new neighbours had learned from their parents, our own claim to those skills having skipped a generation or more.

I continued to do things the hard way; I think by then my love of finding out just how much could be accomplished with only basic tools, natural resources or reclaimed materials, pluck, and determination was more important to me than actually getting things done. Eventually we tried living in our own home, though we had only completed floors and walls and windows. Our shake roof did not leak, but snow did sift in, and though we had the biggest woodstove anyone had ever seen, there were times when a cup of water in the same small room would form a skim of ice. Fortunately the north coast does not have severe cold weather for very long. More frightening was the way the entire house would shimmy with the gale-force winds through those long winter nights. However, the charm of receiving guests to our home as the tide came in, knowing they would stay for hours until the water receded, is unforgettable.

While working in Oona River, I brought my plans for building a shelter for the salmon enhancement site for the men to review, and they approved them. I felt the pride of my own pioneering ancestors gathered behind me in that moment. Our crew spent that summer constructing the buildings, splitting shakes by hand, pouring a concrete dam, laying a water line, clearing trails and avoiding barking spiders. When I think of all we accomplished I realize that I must have driven that crew hard, but I remember no complaints. We were united in our commitment to making good on this rare job opportunity, with funding provided by the federal government to support salmon enhancement efforts in our part of the coast. When we finished the Porcher Island projects we commissioned someone to take us across Ogden Channel to Mud Bay, where we hiked up a fabulously rushing and tumultuous river to clear trails for salmon monitoring. Wet, wet, cold, and still more wet, we relied on all our best survival skills to build the fires we needed to make cowboy coffee. When one of our young hires from town snuck away with the chainsaw to cut down a huge tree, just for the heck of it, we were too exhausted to express much more than our general disgust and disappointment.

Eventually, I concluded that raising our kids in a place where they could fish for trout off our doorstep and ice skate at the beaver dam was not enough to offset the fact that we were not earning more than a subsistence living from our crab fishing. After Lou Allison and I spearheaded a community effort to prevent the helicopter spraying of Round Up in the watershed above Oona River, a campaign that took me into town more frequently that summer, I worked up a resumé and applied for some jobs in Prince Rupert. I was offered a position at Scott, Vohora, Chartered Accountants, over the Surf Club. Eventually, I had a third child, Brendan. My husband, who was now working for B.C. Ferries, was away more than he was home, and when he finally moved to Vancouver to pursue another career, we divorced.

Once I felt free of an unhappy marriage I found the true depths of loneliness. I climbed out of them to correct my childhood mistake of quitting dance lessons when I got my first pair of glasses. Ella at Spectrum City Dance knew that adults wanted to dance too, so I started in jazz dance, and then got to try some ballet and musical theater with other schools. My Leo nature flourished whenever I had a chance to perform on stage, and it all came together in the community production of "Leader of the Pack." Was it only three performances? Live theatre, live music: it's all around us, but the immediacy of the experience in Rupert was unparallelled.

When I became the accountant for the Friendship House Association of Prince Rupert and began to get to know some native people, I closed the circle on my college studies in cultural anthropology, abandoned when I realized that aboriginals were able to fully interpret and represent themselves. In these years I did a tremendous amount of canoeing, including midnight moonlight paddles and a four-day trip down the Skeena from Terrace to the docks in Prince Rupert. I saw more of the wild country around Prince Rupert than in the whole preceding decade.

A few years later, I was thrilled to get a call out of the blue from Dan Miller, then North Coast Member of the Legislative Assembly, asking if I was interested in a job as his executive assistant. Always politically active, I was honoured to be in a position both to represent government interests in the riding, and to take local concerns back to the M.L.A. However, when Dan decided not to seek re-election, my job was over. With the value of properties in Prince Rupert plummeting and both my older children now in the lower mainland, I sold the house and everything in it and by Christmas 2000, Brendan and I were gone. After 25 years away, I returned to Portland, Oregon, where I work at a desk and visit the mountains and the beach on holidays.

My clearest memories of life on the north coast are waterlogged: rowing across the Prince Rupert harbour in a daily commute; retrieving a car seat from the salt chuck under the Dodge Cove dock, presumably tossed over by someone irritated with it taking up dock space, and watching it rust before my eyes; singing "Farewell to Nova Scotia" at the top of my lungs into the weather while hauling crab gear, dressed head to toe in Helly Hansen; Jeannine's wide open eyes under the water as she was hauled back to the surface, still clinging firmly to her tricycle; midnight canoe adventures; crossing the Skeena to the hot springs; swimming in Diana Lake every single day of the summer of 2000. Those are the milestones of my life.

Acclimatization

by Chloe Beam

WHY PRINCE RUPERT?

Growing up in farming country north of Lake Erie, my formative years were marked by lightning strikes and harrowing charges from cows, bulls, geese and guinea hens. I attained my B.A. in history during the murky depths of the American invasion of Vietnam. My partner was an American draft dodger. He was arrested and served time in the Don Jail, Toronto for carrying an anarchist flag in a protest march against the U.S. invasion of Cambodia, where he was clubbed by a riot cop and then charged with assaulting an officer. I wanted to escape to the peace of nature after reading *Pilgrim at Tinker Creek* by Annie Dillard and Henry David Thoreau's *Walden*. In 1977, we travelled to the end of the road.

✧ ✧ ✧ ✧

Gunk Holing in Boats

In Prince Rupert we landed jobs as group home parents. One particularly drama-filled full moon night all our teenagers went A.W.O.L. It was then my partner and I decided to adopt a more relaxed lifestyle. We had met a group of activists opposing the northern pipeline project. Some of them were fishermen and net menders who were squatting in Salt Lakes. They told us about the vacant cabins there; we could have a rustic cabin right on the ocean. All we needed was our own dinghy to get across the harbour.

We located a beautiful wooden lapstrake dinghy which we bottom painted and christened *Wife of Bath*. We also bought a canoe. We had more money than common sense at that point. We loaded all our belongings into *Wife of Bath* and all our house plants into the canoe, which we towed behind the dinghy. This was our very first trip across the harbour and we were loaded almost to the gunwales. We left Function Junction, thinking it didn't look that far across to Salt Lakes. We were excited about our new lifestyle. Our cat, Artaud, walked along the edge of the gunwales to show us how relaxed he was. When the canoe came close, Artaud jumped in. Once we got away from shore we realized we had a generous swell coming on our beam. About halfway across the harbour, it became clear our seagull engine was having trouble making forward progress against the strong headwinds. The waves were higher now. Then the house plants shifted. The canoe lurched to one side and immediately began filling with water. Artaud got a dunking and howled in dismay; I rescued him. Helplessly, we watched the canoe fill with saltwater. It had built-in flotation, so it didn't sink entirely. We didn't want to cut her loose, even though she became a drag anchor. Now we were making no headway at all. We were, however, making amazing leeway. We watched the entrance to Salt Lakes disappear as we were dragged further and further down the wilderness side of the harbour. By now, we realized that the harbour was vast and a small boat can run into all sorts of trouble. We did manage to land on a somewhat hospitable shore about five miles down from Salt Lakes. My partner tied the canoe up to a tree. We would come back for that later. Meanwhile I was in the water keeping *Wife of Bath* from going high and dry on the falling tide. We were all of us wet and mildly hypothermic. Thankfully, the seagull started and we made it to Salt Lakes and unloaded our belongings. That was our start to life on the waters of Prince Rupert's harbour.

Life was good on the north coast. During one really low tide, Bill took us abalone fishing out near Triple Island. We washed up to the rocks in a small dinghy, quickly prying the nacreous shells off the rocks before they suctioned down irretrievably. Then, heaving our bounty bag home, we pounded, smoked and canned them.

I had never eaten so well. Our larders were full of canned salmon, pickled herring and smoked fish. The local fishermen were generous; there was always a Skeena River salmon for the feast nights. Stewart, the sax player,

termed us "the Busheoise." We ate so
many crabs that I became quite blasé
about them. Years later, in a fish shop
in downtown Toronto, pregnant and
craving crab, I would break down
into heaving sobs: the crabs cost $18
each, and looked mossy and old.

Crossing the harbour in an open
skiff was always an adventure. Prince
Rupert is famous for southeast-
ers, with driving rain and gale force
winds. After we had moved into our
cottage at Crippen Cove, we pro-

*Chloe in
Heathen, 1982.*

cured an old Wahl Brothers 20-foot skiff with an inboard antique Vivian
marine engine, complete with flywheel start. This was our storm boat.
We called it *Joe's Lunch*. It announced its presence by its distinctive, slow
heartbeat, putt putt putt. We sold *Wife of Bath* and bought a sturdier carvel
dinghy named *Heathen*. My partner and I were the type who subscribed to
Wooden Boat magazine. No tough efficient bulldozer of an aluminium
skiff for us.

One peaceful starry night we rowed out to check our crab pot. As
I dipped the oars in the sea, a swirl of light trailed behind. What was
that? Was I hallucinating? White tracings reflected in the water. I hadn't
heard of the miracle of phosphorescence, apparently caused by dinofla-
gellates, tiny sea creatures that emit luciferin. Even the scientific explana-
tion sounds magical.

One time I was coming home from Casey Cove with a precious cargo
of sockeye salmon. I was rowing that day as my engine was in repair. A
seal kept following me. He arched out of the water and repeatedly tried
to grab the fish right out of my dinghy. I finally had to hit him with an
oar, not hard, just hard enough to show him who was boss.

My favourite activity was beachcombing, with firewood the main prize.
The triumph of prying a huge log into the sea, with a tool called a peavey,
and towing it home behind my little skiff, made me feel positively trium-
phant.

I never knew what strange things I would find washed up on the shore.

One time a section of the B.C. Ferries dock washed up right in front of our cottage during a gale-wracked night. It was quite a surprise in the morning to find ourselves completely hidden behind this behemoth. We were overjoyed at the free timber it presented, but a helicopter soon flew over. Not long after, a tugboat crew arrived and towed it back to Rupert where it was fastened more securely to once again serve the ferry. Another time, scrambling along the shore, I was startled to see a perfectly intact eyeball with sky blue eye, sitting on a rock, unblinkingly staring.

Another eye-opener was just how lost one could get in Prince Rupert's harbour in the fog. I was returning from a day long run up the Skeena to Terrace. I had a cardboard box full of baby chicks, which had just been wrested from a comforting heat lamp. I had a compass, but what was my bearing to Crippen? After what seemed like hours alone in the dark, damp, enclosing fog, I could hear shore echoes. Through the veil of fog, a land mass suddenly loomed up. I shut off my engine. I could still hear "peep peep peep." Good! The chicks are still alive. I called out hoping there would be some dog or human to respond. Instead, I discerned a very clear "Baaaaah." Where was I? Aha! The only ungulates that baa are on AniAn Island in the middle of Metlakatla Pass, just past the mouth to Crippen. I called out louder and heard Barney, my neighbour's dog, barking from Crippen Cove. Thanks Barney, for guiding me home.

There was a sudden storm that hit in the fall of 1984. I was coming home from a supply run to town when the harbour was transformed into angry boiling surf. *Heathen* was skiing furiously down mountains of waves. As I hit the trough I had to grasp the tiller with all my strength and concentrated fear to keep from ploughing into the wave in front of me. This was a treacherous, fatal storm that took the lives of many fishermen and women out on the sea, friends whom we had tree planted with, partied with, heard legends about. The sea occasionally reminds us of just how fragile and ephemeral we are.

There were many stories of drowning over the years I was in Rupert, some happening right before our eyes. Soon after we arrived in Prince Rupert around 1978, there was a famous Hallowe'en party at Function Junction. The costumes were over the top. There was a net-entangled mermaid who had an impressive fish tail with tin cans and a rubber boot snagged on it, and, outrageously, a Ku Klux Klan member, who burned a cross right on the Function Junction docks. Unfortunately, a young man who had just arrived in Rupert fell off the docks that night and drowned. No one noticed. That was the last party held there.

That same year another young new arrival, late at night, overturned his boat at the mouth of Salt Lakes. He drowned before we could get to him. We brought him in to the cabin next door and laid him on the porch until the authorities could be notified the next day. All night there was audible groaning as his body emptied of air.

Another time, a fisherman, out on Hecate Straight, saw what he thought was a seal swimming in the surf. Through the sights of his rifle, he realized what he was looking at was a human floating in a wet suit. He pulled the unconscious man out of the water, saving him. He was an abalone diver named Jake, whose boat had drifted away, leaving him stranded for countless hours. Jake did not dive alone after that; he went out with an experienced abalone diver a year later and did not return. He just did not surface. This fisherman sold his boat and left the area after that. He had enough of abalone fishing.

These are the sobering truths of living on the sea, especially the cold rough waters of the north. We all know many tragic stories.

  ✣   ✣   ✣   ✣

The Coastal Community

When you live on an island accessible only by boat, the other mariners become your community. There were no yachts, only working boats used for hauling, transportation and fishing, operated by an independent, resourceful group of co-operative individuals. At first some of the established fishermen of Dodge Cove dismissed some of us newcomers as hippies. Eventually, inroads and infatuations occurred and everyone lived happily ever after.

The parties were sensational. In the spring, coinciding with the herring run, we celebrated the Erotic Poetry contest, an organized event with a rented hall, a bar and much rhyming, risqué revelations and revelry. Some of the poems were classic. One of Ghislaine's poems was a metaphor that compared making love to making yoghurt.

In the fall, when the fishermen and mushroom pickers returned, loaded with their bounty, we would gather for potluck dinners and dance all night to The Squeeze, The Clash, the Stones, The Pretenders, Elvis Costello, Peter Gabriel. One standout housewarming party took place in Crippen Cove. The hostess had just that day, at great trouble, hauled a brand new Ikea sofa across the harbour and up the rocks. It was a small cabin and a big sofa. We were all nicely fed and dancing to Marian Faithful. Suddenly, someone started to spew vomit all over the new sofa. She ran for the porch, straight through the dancers. The blissful dancers became aware of a warm wet, viscous, sour smelling material covering our arms, shoulders, hair and feet. Even the cat was bathed in vomit. It became known as the Vomit Party. The sofa was never the same.

✻   ✻   ✻   ✻

Two Roberts

There were two Roberts based in Crippen Cove when I was there. One Robert wore colourful hats and was well liked by everyone. We gave the other Robert a wide berth as he had once chased a neighbour, threatening him with an axe. Both Roberts met violent endings. The well-respected Robert was shot by an unknown sniper while vacationing on a remote beach on the big island of Hawaii. It was over a year before the sniper was caught. Robert's family was devastated.

Before his death, Robert had told his closest kin that he had invested in silver and buried it in a metal box on his property. There had been a ferocious gale that winter, which had knocked down several huge spruce trees on Robert's property. Robert's mom, dad and sister flew out from Oshawa for a week and sadly went through his belongings. They spent days cleaning up the fallen trees and going over the ground with a metal detector, in an attempt to find the buried silver. They left without it. My woodstove was right beside a window that overlooked Robert's workshop, across the stream. One day as I sat warming my feet, it occurred to me that a man's workshop is his refuge, and, maybe, that was where Robert had buried his treasure. At low tide I crept under his workshop. It was dark under there. At the back where the pilings ended and the building extended onto the land, there was a cavity. I stuck my hand in and immediately felt a metal box. I hauled it home and opened it. Sure enough, this was Robert's silver. I notified the family, and then had it couriered to them.

The other volatile Robert wasn't around much. He had started framing a huge pyramid near Bennett's Point and then abandoned it. He left to go gold panning in the Yukon. He had a claim on Bonanza Creek near Dawson City. There, he became known as Two-by-Four Bob, because that is what he used to attack a fellow patron at Diamond Tooth Gertie's Gambling Casino in Dawson City. In 2005 we read that Robert had been fatally shot on the property next to his claim, in an argument over gold.

✱   ✱   ✱   ✱

The Year of the Wolves

When Ridley Island, across from Digby Island, was blasted flat to build a giant coal terminal in 1982, Digby Island suddenly became overpopulated with wolves. They must have swum across the harbour entrance. People in Dodge Cove and Crippen Cove started to lose their pets and livestock to wolves. Pigs were disappearing, chickens, dogs, a turkey, my cat Oedipuss, all haplessly snatched in the night.

My neighbour Bill woke up one night to hear his dog Barney groaning and crying outside. He looked out the upstairs window and saw a wolf shaking Barney by the throat. Bill shouted and rushed to the scene. Fortunately Barney lived, but his vocal chords were severed and he couldn't bark anymore. This caused him to lose his position as head dog in the Cove to young upstart Tosh. Or maybe the trauma of such overwhelming force being exerted on him by a superior canine caused him to lose his self-esteem and drop in status.

I was annoyed with the wolves. I lost my rooster, four chickens, a cat, and a whole boatload of rotten fish. I had spent a great deal of time digging these rotten fish, from a fisherman's spoiled catch, into the soil of my garden in the late summer. Every morning in the winter, I would go out to the garden to see huge craters where the wolves had excavated another helping of the decomposing fish. Drat!

Wolves are exquisite creatures, however, and late one November night I was to have one of my most memorable experiences. I lived in a small cabin on pilings on a clamshell midden beach. There was an outhouse out back close to the woods, but often when I woke up in the night, I would leave the loft and go down to the beach to pee. It was brighter and I knew my way down. The lapping of the water was comforting. As

I stepped outside on the deck this particular night, I was astounded by the brightness. I looked up and beheld undulating dripping curtains of aurora borealis filling the entire sky. I decided to walk down to the point to get a panoramic view. I had just seated myself on the rocks of the point to enjoy the electromagnetic spectacle, when from the next point over, a pack of wolves started to howl. At first it was intermittent. Then the wolves got into full swing. They bayed and chorused, sometimes in unison, sometimes in solo arias, calling down the northern lights to dance and snap in rhythm. I still get shivers down my spine whenever I think about the unearthly amazing sound of that biophony accompanied by the celestial light show.

A wolf is so unmistakably not a dog. I was walking on the old boardwalk, that the Japanese internment prisoners built during the Second World War, through the muskeg, from Crippen Cove to Dodge Cove. In broad daylight, I startled a wolf out from under the boardwalk. He must have been sleeping there. He looked like he had bed-head. He loped out right under me. We were two feet apart, looking at each other. His eyes drilled into mine. They were the wildest most haunting green eyes I have ever seen. I screamed and he ran off. I was not really frightened, as I knew from reading Farley Mowat that wolves do not attack humans. (Well, maybe a little frightened).

*   *   *   *

I used to say I moved away from Prince Rupert because I had grown tired of the C.B.C. (I listen to it exclusively now, by the way.) It was probably the weather. There is so little sun in Prince Rupert, people's skin is blue-white. Even the creosote hydro poles have moss all over them. On average, it rains in Rupert 250 days of the year. I am one of those rare people on Vancouver Island who never complain if it rains. In fact, in my opinion, it doesn't rain enough here. That is the great teaching of Prince Rupert: it acclimatizes you to the reality of rain and the value of community co-operation. Thank you, Prince Rupert, for all these cherished memories.

Turned Inside Out

by Helen Heffernan

THE STORY OF HOW I came to build a cabin on a north coast island in B.C. starts in a tiny room in Toronto. With a bed under the eaves and a maple scratching at the window, the room I rented in the heart of Toronto when I started university was in keeping with the snow caves I'd built against fences and the wattle huts I'd woven deep in the woods, my solitary child-hood retreats. The room came with none of the restrictions of residence life or the demands of co-op living. There was a hot plate outside the door, a shared bathroom down the hall and, on the first floor, a commu-nal telephone. When I phoned my parents to tell them about the rooming house, their skepticism surprised me.

The inhabitants of the house were all older than Moses to me. I wiled away hours piecing together their histories, imagining war torn Europe in the upheaval in the landlady's eyes, and a windswept prairie in the slow steps of the old man in the room beneath me. I measured his solitude against my own and feared the vector of my life would parallel his. Some-times, when I left the house, I saw him, shoulders sloped, face a blur of age, staring out the window.

The street, Chicora Avenue, was a relief, the breeze a cool kiss of rec-ognition. I knew how to find companionship in the wind's monologue, in the dance of sunlight on wet pavement, in the slow rot of autumn leaves underfoot. But at the university, my isolation showed. As other students chatted in hallways, I'd hover. Back in my room, I felt muffled, invisible, like a lake under the snows of winter. Loneliness had been a formless presence in my rural home but in the big city, it stalked me. It was 1971, Bob Dylan and Joni Mitchell were on the radio, Woodstock was still in the air, but where were all the freedom loving fun-seekers?

Right under my nose, as it turned out. Carole, a long-lost childhood friend, and her musician husband, were renting a third floor apartment in a house just across the street. A party house. In an instant, I joined their nightlong jam sessions, drinking beer by the caseload, smoking and singing my heart out, strumming with the others on a guitar. I met my future husband in that house: Norm, all golden curls and lithe limbs, Miles Davis on the sax in the background. From the built-in window seat in the flat, Norm and I often studied the glowing night city below, sharing a mutual sense of doom about urban life, among other things.

During that time, Norm came and went, fishing on the west coast for a living, studying music in the city. Whenever he showed up, I'd dig out from an avalanche of books and join the party. Eventually, without telling my parents, we moved in together. I remember the long hallway of our second floor Robert Street apartment, how it funnelled the wind from the front windows to the back window, how the rats danced in the attic whenever we played our rented harpsichord, how the smell of desiccated shark soup from below made me gag. By then, Norm worked as a pipe organ tuner; I was a substitute teacher. Our Chicora friends had dispersed; good jobs were scarce. We took to walking arm-in-arm through the night streets, Norm kicking the flaps of his long black coat, our footsteps in sync as we marched past the garbage-gagged fences and the trashed-out buildings of our forlorn neighbourhood. Over and over we discussed the idea of abandoning professional ambition and leaving the city altogether.

During my third pregnancy (I kept the first two, both miscarriages, a secret), my parents, who'd discovered our co-habitation, insisted we marry. When I explained that Norm and I viewed marriage and its promise of monogamy as an irrelevant folly, my parents stepped up the pressure. I miscarried again, but it was too late, the guests had been invited. I have a photo of Paul, Norm's friend from the fishing grounds, yawning during the speeches. Back then, Paul's eyes were like excavators, unearthing the impulse to rebel. He told us about his friends, escapees from cities and career treadmills, inhabiting abandoned cabins in Salt Lakes, a squatters' paradise across the harbour from Prince Rupert. So after the trauma of our wedding, we hitchhiked to the west coast to see for ourselves.

Bathed in unprecedented sunshine that summer, protected on three sides by coastal wilderness, Salt Lakes buzzed with people balanced beautifully on the fulcrum between youth and adulthood, enjoying a moment outside the confines of conformity. Small skiffs came and went by day, and at night people gathered to feast on fresh salmon, crab and homemade huckleberry pies. Salt Lakes enchanted me; its pull was irresistible.

Back in Toronto, the bleakness of the urban landscape was unrelenting. By Christmas, we'd quit our jobs, given away our furniture, returned the harpsichord, and said our good byes. In January 1978, wrapped in blankets, we set off in Norm's drafty, old car, driving through the sobering limbo that is Canada in winter. Days later, we skidded along the wet Skeena highway and into rollicking Prince Rupert.

Paul had the salvaging rights to a dockside warehouse in Prince Rupert. He was showing us the place when his friends, wielding crowbars and hammers, descended like a flock of seagulls. They yanked nails from floorboards, wrenched up the plywood sub floor, levered the siding off the walls, lifted lattice windows from the frames. Others worked on the dock, bundling the salvaged material for towing. A man named Dale, pulling nails with his prosthetic hook, gave me a crowbar and showed me how to use it, smiling at my clumsy efforts. As I worked alongside him, a sea breeze cooled my face and the smiles of a million wavelets filled my peripheral vision.

Helen & Norm climb aboard the Martha Washington.

That winter, at the bar, we talked, danced and drank with a wild array of people: loggers and fishermen, both aboriginal and white, backpackers, draft evaders, and young professionals doing their stint in the north. Norm quickly landed a deckhand job for the herring season. Take along a survival suit, a fisherman advised; guard it with your life. After the fleet left, I curled around Norm's spot in our bed, listened to the winter wind toss rain against the pane and worried for his life. I also landed my first real teaching position, starting in September. Ten days later, Norm, having earned more money than I would make in a year of teaching, returned safely. Pockets fat with cash, the fishermen took over town, celebrating like Roman emperors.

With the spring equinox came the high tides. For several rainy nights Norm helped Paul tow bundles of the salvaged warehouse across the harbour to Crippen Cove and Salt Lakes. Leaving after dark, they timed it so they could float the bundles high up the beach and tie them to overhanging boughs. Paul knew of an abandoned caravan in Crippen Cove. Save rent money, live in the caravan, he suggested. We travelled in Paul's skiff to Digby Island, tugged the skiff up a muddy beach, waded through a mantle of seaweed, climbed a rocky bank and found the caravan deep in the forest. With a come-along and rollers, we inched the rectangular six-by-ten-foot box through the woods and across a stream while the crows, rambunctious with spring fever, jeered in the trees. Paul had a government lease adjacent to Crippen Cove and that's where we set the caravan down, just above a secluded bay.

When we moved into the caravan, sword ferns were springing up from under winter's weight and the moss in the crotches of alders was softening to neon green velvet. Tiny pink blossoms broke out all over the salmonberries' blanched stems and skunk cabbage poked up from the muskeg, unfurling leaves the size of welcome mats. Against heavy skies and from every thicket, balloon-chested song sparrows proclaimed themselves the new poets and a pair of bald eagles led the way in nesting, carrying sticks and seaweed into the branches of the cedar leaning over the bay.

The caravan sat under evergreens that flicked their wet tips in the wind, making a constant patter on its flat roof. All bed at one end, a camp stove and basin at the other, there was just enough room in between for an airtight stove. While *Martha Washington* tugged at the mooring in the bay, the sea stormed and Norm and I cocooned, content with our books, our retreat from life.

Our first visitor, Paul, squeezed into our caravan, his yellow sou'wester dripping. Warming his hands over the airtight, he proposed a generous deal: if Norm and I built a cabin on his lease, we could have it. The cabin had to be built, he explained, or the lease forfeited. The government required 600 square feet, a shed roof would do, no need for wiring and plumbing. We could use the flooring, windows and siding of the salvaged warehouse sitting in bundles on the beach below. He'd help when he could. We'd have it built in no time. Norm and I looked at each other, bouncing a ball of enthusiasm between us.

Helen at the job site of the cabin-building project at Crippen Cove.

We hiked the lease, Paul pointing out the potential view of sea and snow-capped mountains. After he'd gone, Norm climbed one hundred feet up a hemlock, hauling a chain saw. Near the top, he yanked the starter cord and sank the teeth of the saw into the tree. When the top of the tree crashed down through its own branches, he ducked, clinging monkey-like to the trunk. He tied a rope at the cut, shimmied down the tree, and sawed a wedge at the base. We tugged on the tree until we heard cracking, then dropped the rope and ran for our lives. The thump of that first hemlock when it hit the ground was terrifying. Trembling, Norm winced up at the space where it had stood. The trees, like a silent army, seemed to link arms.

Balanced on the fallen tree, Norm amputated branches and I dragged them away. Some of the branches lay beneath the trunk like fingers bent back at the joint and when Norm cut them, the tree dropped closer to the ground, taking him and the screaming chainsaw with it. It was dangerous. I doubt we had even a bandage on hand. Norm proceeded as if he knew what he was doing but, demoted to helpmate, I listened for Paul's skiff, as if he could reason away the deadliness of the endeavour.

When Paul finally did arrive, trees crisscrossed the building site like a giant's game of pick-up-sticks. Rolling a car tire up the pathway, he whistled and laughed at our scratched hands and faces. Fire starter, he explained, dousing the tire with oil and stepping back to toss a lit match. For days after that, working in a constant downpour, we heaved house-high branches onto the burn pile, ducking black ribbons of smoke, sweating in our rain gear. One night, we sat by the inferno and Paul talked about the back-to-the-land movement, conferring upon our cabin-building its righteous convictions. He mentioned starting a land co-op on Porcher Island, which made great sense to me. But Norm sat with his legs hugged into his chest, exhausted and perhaps regretting what he'd got himself into.

Our cabin-building took on an irrational urgency, as if the race of our pioneering forefathers against winter's arrival was part of our genetic makeup. All through June we rose at dawn and worked until midnight, skidding one rainy day into the next. Alongside us, the fire worked too, devouring brush piles, spurning downpours, and mimicking our moods, a hissing gobbler by day, a smouldering eye by night, a dull heap of ash at dawn. After clearing the site, we hacked through the webbed roots in the forest floor, digging holes for the pilings. Every night, water seeped into the holes and in the morning, while I held his legs and suppressed laughter, Norm hung down the holes and bailed them out, cursing.

From over in Crippen Cove came the occasional, reassuring screech of Bill and Shelley's chainsaw. They'd been around the north coast longer and knew more about everything. When Bill showed up, we were on the beach, trying to budge the huge railway ties we'd beachcombed to use as pilings. We had to get them up to the building site. Bill fetched a block and tackle and showed us how to string it from high in a tree down to the beach. After he left, we spent hours leaping up and hanging together on the rope, lengthening our arms as we gradually inched the sodden ties up to the holes we'd dug.

In the evenings, I'd pump up the camp stove and measure rice and rainwater into the orange cast iron pot I'd brought from Toronto. We started running low on food and fuel but we put off a trip to town, not wanting to lose time on our project. Luckily, when the sun finally emerged, so did common sense. We set off for town at dawn, hauling a plywood skiff over knee-deep seaweed. I remember the rich smell of that sun-warmed seaweed and the delicate quiet of the sea as it tongued the mucky shoreline. Feeding ducks lifted into the air as we putted across the summer sea. In the bow, I warmed my face in the rare sun. Norm, one knee on the tiller, stripped off his rain gear.

In town, we looked at each other and laughed. Norm's hair had turned Afro, a beard hid his jaw, and bent glasses framed eyes gone slightly wild. We bought our supplies, then headed to the bar to join a table of other cabin-feverish people, many as unsuited to their projects as we were. Over a glass of beer, hardship morphs into something more glamorous.

But the reality of blackened fingers, bruised shins and sore muscles returned in an instant back on Digby Island. Shouldering planks up from the beach, our footsteps jarred; the echoes of our separate hammer blows on the floor joists collided in the treetops.

"Take full swings, don't tap like a goddamn woodpecker," Norm said.

"Fuck off!" I yelled.

Civility, once taken for granted between us, was sacrificed on the altar of our subfloor.

On the beach, the salvaged plywood was already separating. Norm wiped the slugs off a sheet and laid it across my back, showing me how to catch the bottom edge with one hand and reach over my shoulder to grab the top edge. The span was difficult; the wet plywood bowed my head as I carried it up the pathway. Like Jesus with his cross, I thought. But humour, like a renegade soldier, had all but deserted us.

That July, the sun appeared just three or four times, but its arrival inspired us to drop our tools, strip off our rain gear and head to Salt Lakes for a swim. When we got there, the Tarzan rope was in full swing, naked white bodies draped the shoreline, and swimmers splashed in the lake. Nothing cleans like a cold lake after weeks without a bath; nothing satisfies like a floating dock in the sunshine with friends, beer, and maybe a joint or two passed between wet fingers.

In August, one storm after another came in off the ocean and found every mistake we had made in the framing. Still, we did finally get the walls raised, the roof on, the sea-scratched windows set in place. Sometimes, while Norm persevered, I retreated to the beach, squatted on a platter of slate and watched the barnacles in the rush and retreat of waves. Sea and sky had bonded on the grey horizon, there was fresh snow in the mountains: winter was coming.

So was my first teaching job. Two days before school started, I checked in. The teachers asked if I was even going to decorate my classroom. Preoccupied by cabin building, I'd forgotten the details of running an elementary classroom. That first year of teaching was a steep learning curve for me. The daily commuting across the harbour didn't make it easier. Meanwhile Norm worked alone, finishing the cabin.

A frantic year of teaching and commuting by boat passed, then another. While I withstood what is now termed sexual harassment at work, Norm was unapologetic about sleeping with another woman. And though monogamy, as I explained, was not something I expected, it turned out that infidelity works like a magnet, drawing flaws into a heap. There's more to the story of course, but the glimmer of the god I'd once seen in Norm faded, our marriage unravelled, he left Prince Rupert, and I found myself alone in the cabin, as alone as I'd been in my room under the eaves. Blame it on the tangling salal, the circling sea, the unbroken wilderness. The city would never have turned us so thoroughly inside out.

Coastal Quilting

by Kristin Miller

I MOVED TO SALT LAKES in 1981 to live alone in the slow aftermath of a splintering marriage. We had come to Prince Rupert in 1978, and married in 1980, buying a ramshackle cabin at Salt Lakes as a honeymoon getaway. We bartered a quilt for half the purchase price of a sturdy Davidson lifeboat skiff, imagining romantic voyages and candlelight evenings in the little cabin without electricity. When our life together unravelled within the year, the cabin became my refuge. Although I was ambivalent about leaving my husband, we both understood when I packed away my electric sewing machine, bought an old Singer treadle machine, and asked him to hoist it aboard the skiff.

Arlo, a stalwart terrier mutt, moved across the harbour with me, balancing easily in the bow with his front feet up on the gunwales and his tail flying in the wind. He chased otters and seagulls on the beach, and stole hot dogs from the neighbors. The dog revelled in this wild new life, while I settled in with trepidation. I was determined to live alone and take care of myself, but there was a lot I needed to learn, and fast.

On one of my first solo trips to town, I found a drowned woman, floating face down. I grabbed her by the collar and pulled her head above water, but then I couldn't manoeuvre the boat so I yelled at a passing fishboat for help. The fisherman climbed into my skiff, but wouldn't touch the body. He left me holding it while he steered my boat to the dock. This unnerving experience guaranteed that I always kept my lifejacket zipped tight and my emergency whistle close at hand.

Salt Lakes was a tiny community of a dozen cabins and shacks on a cove across the harbour from Prince Rupert. The lake was inland. The cabins had been built as holiday homes in the fifties, but now they were derelict and inhabited by maritime back-to-the-landers, hard-drinking hermits, hippie fishermen, and adventurous women. The cabins sold for a modest sum: mine cost $3,500, but that didn't include the land it was on. I paid $70 a year to lease the land.

I treadled my way in dim light through countless quilting projects, ironing the seams with a six-pound flatiron my Grandma had used as a girl. The skiff and the treadle sewing machine became the most useful and valued objects in my new life. The skiff was seaworthy, but the outboard motor was cranky and obstinate, and seemed almost hypochondriacal in the way it would break down if I was nervous crossing the harbour in the dark.

I was nervous about everything. I feared big storms and getting lost in the fog. I worried about exploding propane tanks, about almost being broke, about cutting off my leg with the chainsaw, about poisoning myself with the unrefrigerated food I kept cooling in the creek.

But my greatest fear was that I couldn't have children. After years of trying, I had finally gotten pregnant the previous winter, but had suffered terrible pain diagnosed as morning sickness until I collapsed and almost died from a rare complication of an ectopic pregnancy. I lost the baby along with my health and my emotional stability, so I was in precarious shape, weepy and weak, when I moved across the harbour.

Kristin's dog Arlo stands on a boardwalk in front of her cabin at Salt Lakes.

I was helped and befriended by the small community living there, and comforted by the slow momentum of life in this odd maritime outpost. If my neighbors sensed my frailty and sadness, they responded by chopping my firewood or inviting me to dinner.

Lorrie, Linda, and Margo and their partners had three

cabins in a row across from me, on the lively side of the cove, and Arlo and I would often hike around the cove at low tide to visit, or row across to the makeshift dock. The three women often worked together — making jam, chopping and stacking firewood, canning salmon in gigantic jittering pressure cookers. Lorrie sliced rounds of fish, Linda filled the jars, and Margo monitored the gauges and the heat to maintain a constant pressure.

Linda's mom had given her a subscription to Chatelaine magazine, and one day we sat at Lorrie's house, joking about the modern household appliances it featured. Lorrie slowly toasted slice after slice of bread on an old cast-iron stove lid, while Linda read out questions from the magazine's stress test quiz. Lorrie and I scored at the "no stress" level, while Linda was 20 points higher due to a planned trip to the tropics. It wasn't that our lives were without stress, it was that the magazine quiz didn't cover any of our worries and dangers.

I had given up my profession as an occupational therapist after my ill-fated pregnancy, feeling unable to help others, and in need of help myself. But when I had regained my health, I worked part-time at a group home for troubled teens, putting in a 48 hour stint every two weeks, which paid as well as a half-time job. If the weather was threatening, I'd leave home a day early to make sure I got to work on time.

I also made quilts to sell or trade. I bartered a quilt for a wood-burning cookstove, and another for a stereo system that ran on a car battery, not realizing I'd have to take the heavy battery to town to charge it up. I traded my sewing and mending skills for repairs to my outboard, firewood, homemade wine, salmon, new windows, and propane lights. I made a quilt for Ginger, who was an apprentice carpenter, and she repaired the sagging underpinnings of my cabin by sistering new joists next to the old ones. I worked with her down in the mud, pondering the meaning of sisterhood as we woman-handled the heavy beams into place.

As friends began to have babies, I taught the women how to make quilts. Each woman added a concentric border, then passed the quilt on to the next person who wanted to work on it. Sometimes we each made separate squares, then spent a day arranging them into a pleasing design. By 1985 we had made a dozen baby quilts together, with perhaps 30 people involved.

I loved the warmth and productivity of our quilting days, but found it painful to listen to the women talking about their babies, pregnancies, and birth experiences. I was very jealous, though careful to keep this feeling hidden. Eventually I realized that I had to change the way I felt, or give up quilting with my friends. I chose to stay in the quilting circle, and was slowly able to reconcile my feelings and let go of my jealousy and bitterness.

Over the years, I became a competent and confident boater, and was now more often exhilarated than frightened in the skiff. I was happily settled into the community at Salt Lakes until my friends began to leave. Linda went travelling, then moved to Vancouver. Margo and her family became caretakers at the C.B.C. transmitter site above Dodge Cove, and Lorrie and Paul bought a house at Crippen Cove. By 1986, most of my other friends had moved on too, leaving a shrunken community of eccentric and heavy-drinking coastal oddballs – and me.

I was in the doldrums, and couldn't decide whether to stay or leave, so compromised by accepting a job as live-in housekeeper at the group home for the winter. I stayed there during the week, and went home on weekends. I had started writing a quilting book at my cabin, but it was difficult without electricity. It was easier in town, especially after I joined the Prince Rupert writers group.

I met Iain at the writers group, and was drawn to his quiet intensity and quick wit. When spring came and I moved back across the harbour, he

Kristin makes a harbour crossing in winter.

would sail over to visit me. He stayed at my cabin when I went away for a few weeks, and I was startled but pleased to find that he had built shelves for me, a settee by the woodstove, and a little writing desk in the corner for himself. Without much discussion, he moved in, and I regained my contentment at Salt Lakes. In the summer we went sailing in his tiny boat, and began to explore the north coast, anchoring in remote coves and being rocked to sleep by the waves, with the mast of the boat like a vertical bundling board between us.

We worked together at a fish farm for a couple years, after the group home closed and Iain tired of being editor of the local paper. Arlo was an ancient dog by then, threadbare and rickety, but still eager for adventure. He wore an old wool sweater, tied tight with a big knot at his back. We held the knot and steered him up and down the boardwalk, and Iain jumped into the frigid salt water twice to rescue Arlo when he fell in. But Arlo still loved boat rides, and we took him along on our first long voyage in Iain's new boat, *Nid*. In rough weather, we packed Arlo tightly in blankets to keep him from sliding around, and I made a sling for hoisting him on and off the boat.

We went south for a month, then spent another month coming back, baking bread in a Dutch oven on lonely beaches, and filling our rubber dinghy with water to wash our clothes. Iain was a natural sailor and at ease on the sea, and I had become more daring and seaworthy myself.

In the fall of 1989, we took over caretaking at the transmitter site while Margo and Hans tried out life in Vancouver. They decided they liked city life, so we stayed on at C.B.C. Hill. We still commuted to town by boat, but had a proper dock now, a tiny A.T.V. to take us up and down the hill, and electricity. We bought a computer and re-entered the modern era. Iain's two books about our boating adventures and misadventures were published and I finished my quilting book.

The quilting circle used the helicopter pad near the radio tower to lay out quilt squares. By 1991 we had finished 23 group-made baby quilts, a wedding quilt for Lorrie and Paul, and a comfort quilt for a friend who had cancer. I suggested that we display our quilts at the art gallery of the Museum of Northern B.C. in Prince Rupert.

At the gallery opening, the room vibrated with the colourful energy of the quilts and the excitement of the quilters and their friends. I was lured away shortly before the festivities began, and when I returned, there was a quilt I had never seen before, stretched on a quilting frame in the middle of the room. My friends had made it for me! Lorrie, Linda, Margo, Shelley, Bill and other friends by then living in Vancouver had made the center, and the northern quilters each made separate squares and sewed the quilt together.

I worked part-time in town as co-ordinator of a mental health activity program, and Iain spent his days writing. We bought a big sailboat my brother had built, and every summer we went sailing for six or eight weeks. I was happily part of a community again; the village of Dodge Cove was 15 minutes away down a beautiful though muddy path through the woods.

Our group now made quilts to commemorate important life events, and mailed quilt squares back and forth to include quilters who had moved south. By 2000, 50 quilts had been made by the ever-expanding circle. A hundred people had participated in making these quilts, some making only a single square, others working on almost all of the quilts. More than a dozen men had taken part, and at least a dozen children had made squares or added stitching or embellishment to the quilts.

In 2000, Iain and I moved to Gabriola Island in southern B.C. He is a prize-winning author now, and I make custom bed quilts, art quilts for exhibitions, and personal quilts that evoke and express my feelings and experiences. I've initiated several activist group-made quilt projects on Gabriola, most recently the UnspOILed Coast Quilt Project, as part of the No Tankers campaign opposing a proposed pipeline from the Alberta tar sands to the north coast. The quilts depict all that is precious on the coast, and we fundraise by covering them with black fabric "oil blobs" and inviting viewers to donate a dollar and take off an oil blob to help keep our coast oil free.

I still make quilts together with my old friends, mailing my contributions back up north, or to Vancouver where Lorrie is the center of a vibrant quilt circle. Lorrie is a grandma now, and so many squares were contributed for her daughter Elisha's baby that two quilts were made for him. Many of the squares came from Elisha's north coast childhood friends. We had made quilts for them when they were babies, and now they are grown up and joining us to make quilts for a new generation.

Our friend Jane periodically organizes what she calls the "Kristinite Challenge," where eight or 10 people each make a center square, which is then passed on so that each participant adds something to each quilt, then passes it on again, until every person has worked on every quilt. Each person receives the large quilt top that has evolved from her small center square.

Our group-made quilts are more sophisticated now, but still express a great depth of meaning. The quilting circle continues to expand, and it is getting harder to count how many people have taken part, or how many quilts we have made. But making quilts together with my friends is the one constant in my life over the past 30 years, and I'm very grateful for the connection.

A quilt is born.

The More Things Change

by Peggy Carl

I NEVER PLANNED TO move up North. One thing just followed another, step by step.

My brother Alan brought his girlfriend down to Victoria for Christmas in 1977. We couldn't read his handwriting so thought of her as Dolly/Polly/Molly. They talked a lot about life in the north and invited me to come stay with them in Crippen Cove. My family looked after my two daughters and fed their father while I was away. I had a wonderful time, despite the fact that it was January and I didn't have proper warm clothing or rain gear. We spent a lot of time in the skiff, beachcombing, picking abalone and rock scallops off reefs, setting crab traps and digging clams. We also visited in Salt Lakes and even spent the night at the Function Junction. That place made a great impression on me. It was perfect. You could tie up your boat to the dock, and to reserve a place to sleep, you just left your sleeping bag where you wanted to crash. That first time I chose the work bench. There was a small heated living room, a kitchen, a hatch in the floor you could raise so you could sweep the dirt down it, and a semi-public bath which you filled with a hose attached to the kitchen tap, which was poked through a hole in the wall to reach the bath. Wonderful. You never knew who would be already staying there. We also made a trip across Chatham Sound to Humpback Bay to visit Fran and Steve; their homestead and their lifestyle made a great impression on me. I was also impressed by all the young women who travelled in boats and anchored them out: they seemed so skilled and confident.

So by the time I got back to Victoria I had already decided to give my husband notice that I was moving on, and that the kids and I would spend the summer at Crippen Cove. In July and August we had drought conditions but in September it rained every day except for two half-days; but I still wanted to return.

It took until March 1978 to get organized, but we got off the ferry with all our worldly goods, including the family dog. We had borrowed a 1964 three-quarter ton pickup with a tall chickenwire cage built to fill the truck box, which took days to pack. Next came the brass bed tied across the back and two trunks riding on the lowered tailgate. We arrived to snow on the ground, and rain. Brother Alan was herring fishing but his friends Malcolm and Tommy brought their boats across the harbour and lots of volunteers helped dump all our stuff on the decks. It was all a big rush because the tide had turned and we had to offload at Toby Point before it was too low to reach the dock. Almost everything got wet, but we survived. The house we were to caretake was quite a distance from the dock, but we got most of our stuff into the house before dark. Neither stove was functional but we got some gear strung up to dry, made ourselves a nest, and got some sleep. Things improved immensely after that!

As soon as possible I retrieved the skiff *Magnolia*, which I had bought from Anneke the previous summer. I learned that it would have been better to get the barnacles off her hull when they were fresh. Someone donated a four horsepower air-cooled outboard motor, and I already had oars so we were all set to go. As our house was on the trail between Crippen and Dodge Coves, I kept the skiff on a tidal clothesline.

My younger daughter Sarah had her sixth birthday party at our new place and lots of kids and their mothers came. I kind of felt like I was in a zoo, but it was a good introduction. I sent my girls to school in Prince Rupert so they went by ferry then bus with the other kids. For many reasons that didn't work for us so we tried correspondence school – no joy there either, so I home-schooled them for the next four years and we did fine. When they went to school later in Victoria they managed to fit right in.

That first spring I managed to get a garden in despite setbacks. In the south, I had been able to plant earlier. I had never heard of the little migratory birds who swooped down in black clouds and ate every seedling in sight. I did better with acquiring livestock. I bartered future eggs and milk for a goat from Sue Staehli. The goat arrived before her shed was ready and I was given a 10 minute lesson on how to milk, the kids falling over laughing at me trying to milk, squirt – long pause – squirt. Of course they learned really easily and always were better at it than I. Next came birds, about 50 of them from a woman who had just moved into town. They were at the other end of the road in Dodge Cove and we spent several evenings making many trips with wheelbarrow loads of birds stuffed into gunny sacks or packed in cardboard boxes. One drake escaped and it was free for at least a week; I'd get phone calls, but he was always long gone before I got there until Tommy threw himself at the duck as it ran by in the boatshed and caught it. I carried the three geese home one by one, body under one arm, and my other hand holding onto the top of the neck so they couldn't bite. Then I got several more goats from Fran, including a young wether named Phillip who belonged to my older daughter, Marion.

Phillip.

There was a smokehouse on the property so I went into the fish smoking business during the summer. The best fish I had ever tasted was smoked by Linda Gibbs and she gave me her recipe. I also learned a lot from others, including Bill, who brought me loads of pinks. John and Finbar brought me dog salmon and paid me for the smoking by bringing me alder wood to burn. I had to get up every four hours to tend the fire, but other than that it was fun.

That fall I took a course on how to mend gillnets and found out how unbelievably cold my feet could get. Over the next few years I earned a fair amount of money hanging and mending nets, but I wasn't brilliant at it.

Once, my family wanted us to come down to Victoria for Christmas, but Marion's pet goat Phillip had been attacked and almost killed by a neighbour's dog, so I said we couldn't come. I got talked into bringing the goat down with us. My brother Alan carried him down to the car deck of the ferry with a ticket lady running after him and shouting, but the crew just ignored her and we made a bed for him on pallets with crew members' jackets as bedding. I set up a manger for him and filled it with cedar boughs and salal, the cook sent down salad leftovers and other food, and the towel lady brought him fresh linen twice a day. I did get an announcement over the P.A. when I was putting the kids to bed: "Would the

The Topo *makes her maiden voyage across Chatam Sound.*

owner of the goat please report to the car deck." Somewhat embarrassing. Phillip had gotten loose and was wandering around getting the tethered dogs all excited. Getting Phillip back up north was also exciting. I was bringing my car back and had Phillip in the back seat with Marion. Sarah sat in front and I had a bale of hay on the roof and a funky trailer behind. We were in the lineup at Swartz Bay for hours but didn't get on the first ferry. I went to the office in tears and explained that I needed to be on the ferry for Prince Rupert, which only ran once a week, and that the next one from Vancouver Island would get to the terminal too late. They did some phoning and the Rupert ferry waited for us; we just drove across the terminal and onto the ferry, they shut the doors after us, and we left.

During the summer of 1980 the kids were with their father, so I went fishing with Tommy. We made a little money, but it was mostly a great learning experience. He had had good teachers and taught me a lot about basic seamanship. In November, I bought a 21-foot wooden sailboat named *Topo*. Another huge new learning experience. Luckily Malcolm mentored me through the beginning and I confined my trials and errors to the harbour. In January 1981 I took off on my maiden voyage: I crossed Chatham Sound to pick Sarah up from Humpback Bay, where she had been staying with Dory Spencer and Skid; then we carried on up through Steven's Pass to Skiakl Bay. I was looking for a place to homestead and soon decided on Isabellachuck on Porcher Island.

During the spring and early summer of 1981, we spent most of our time at Isabellachuck clearing land and preparing to build a house, but circumstances changed and we moved to Simms Bay in the Creek Islands. It was now too late to build, so I bought a tipi from Sue Staehli, one she had made for herself. I cut down and prepared poles, set up the tipi, and we moved in. I had two stoves, a cookstove and a heater, so I put them back to back just inside the entrance so I could use the cookstove as a kitchen counter and heat with the other. Because of the amount of rain, the smoke flaps didn't work well, so I put in a stovepipe and made a huge raincap from heavy canvas. Uncle Buster, who lived across the way, gave me a tent for the goats and I made a tipi around it creating an inner space for the does and their young and an outer space for the bucks.

My brother Alan towed his floathouse out for us before Christmas. He'd tied a red ribbon into a bow on it, making it look gift-wrapped. It had no windows to speak of and one wall was held on with a scotch windlass. On December 31 my lead doe gave birth to a single male kid we named Satu and the only way I could keep them warm was to put a small stove in and let them have the house.

In 1982 I built a barn with lumber that a neighbour milled and delivered to us. The barn was 8-by-15 feet and had a loft and windows but no door at first. We just nailed a piece of plywood across the opening at night and took it off every morning. We spent the next winter in the tipi and were snowed in from about October until April; it even snowed in May. We humans were comfortable but the animals had a hard time of it. Because the vegetation was frozen so long, it had little nutritional value and we only had one kid born who survived that spring. Every day I filled the barn with small trees and lots of salal and we stomped trails so the goats could get exercise, as they couldn't walk in deep snow that was up to their shoulders. In 1983 we finally moved into the floathouse. What a luxury!

Eventually my children moved to Victoria, lived with my relatives, and went to South Park School. They and my sister's kids would come home for the summers and we had a lot of fun but it was hard to part with them in September. After a few years I couldn't do it anymore. So a friend and I loaded the remaining goats into his pickup and drove them to their new home on Quadra Island. We also had my girls plus my Irish Wolfhound with us so it was quite an adventure, especially as we had to milk the does on the side of the highway.

Eventually, I bought a place in Hunts Inlet on Porcher Island which I still own, and lived there for many years. Then music became my main focus so I moved to Dodge Cove, across the harbour from Prince Rupert, and started teaching violin and played with a series of Celtic bands based in Prince Rupert and Terrace. I no longer had goats; instead, I started rescuing ferrets that had been abandoned, were unwanted by their owners, or surplus at local stores. I had up to 17 at one time. After falling off my deck and shattering my knee, I spent three months in a wheelchair and on crutches. It was time for change, so in 2002, I moved into town. I still had my place in Hunts Inlet and still had my boat *Topo*. I lived in Prince Rupert until 2010, when I moved to the Comox Valley.

It took two summers to bring my boat down the coast. The first leg of the journey took me as far as Rivers Inlet where I had to leave *Topo* over the winter. I flew in the next summer, and after waiting for weather for a week in Smith Inlet, I made it across Queen Charlotte Sound in thick fog all the way. Thank God for compasses and G.P.S. I made it as far as Alert Bay where I found a buyer for *Topo*, as I knew I couldn't afford to keep her in the Comox area. A nice guy living on a boat at the dock helped me pack all my stuff into cardboard boxes and then drove me down island, back to Comox. He is also a boat person and an artist and now we are married.

Although I live in the south now I still live on the water. I have boats, animals, gardens, and music is still huge in my life. I guess some things just never change.

Acknowledgements

First, thank you to the 34 women who agreed to delve into their memories, do the work of sorting and sifting, and write with such *brio*. Thanks to Chris Armstrong, our publisher and owner of Muskeg Press, who took a leap of faith with us, helped us with organization and structure, and worked closely with us throughout. Thanks are also due to Lynn McKinster for early help, encouragement, and the questions we used as guidelines for the writers. And thanks to Kathleen Larkin at the Prince Rupert Library for support.

~*Lou Allison*

Index of Authors

Further Reading from Caitlin Press

Women of Brave Mettle: More Stories of the Cariboo Chilcotin
EXTRAORDINARY WOMEN: VOLUME TWO
Diana French

In this much-anticipated second volume in the Extraordinary Women Anthology series, Diana French follows up on *Gumption and Grit* with more stories of the women who have contributed, or who are still contributing, to the vibrant mosaic that is the Cariboo Chilcotin. The area has more than its share of remarkable women, from educators to rodeo stars, doctors to playwrights, administrators to environmentalists, artists to politicians.

987-1-894759-86-1 | $26.95

Gumption and Grit: Women of the Cariboo Chilcotin
EXTRAORDINARY WOMEN: VOLUME ONE
Sage Birchwater

Gumption and Grit is the first in a series that showcases women of BC: their lives, their successes, their history. In 2005 the Williams Lake Women's Contact Society posted a request for pioneer stories of the women of the Cariboo Chilcotin. What they received was an overwhelming number of tales of hard-ship, faith, adversity, endurance and accomplishment. These women were mothers, trappers, schoolteachers, outfitters, ranchers and homesteaders. *Gumption & Grit* contains more than 35 heartfelt and honest stories, which will resonate with the experiences of all women of this land.

978-1-894759-37-3 | $24.95

Journeywoman: Swinging a Hammer in a Man's World
Kate Braid

Since women started working in the trades in the 1970s, very little has been published about their experiences. In this provocative and important book, Kate Braid tells the story of how she became a carpenter in the face of skepticism and discouragement. Told with humour, compassion and courage, *Journeywoman* is the true story of a groundbreaking woman finding success in a male-dominated field.

978-1-894759-87-8 | $24.95

All Roads Lead to Wells: Stories of the Hippie Days
Susan Safyan

In the late 1960s and '70s a small group of idealistic young women and men, self-described as "volunteer peasants," moved to the tiny town of Wells in British Columbia's Central Interior. *All Roads Lead to Wells* tells the story of these young settlers, their migration, their values, the unexpected friendships forged between the town's old-timers and newcomers and the inevitable clash—occasionally violent—of generations and cultures.

978-1-894759-76-2 | $26.95